Complete Horoscope

2021

Monthly astrological forecasts for every Zodiac sign for 2021

TATIANA BORSCH

Translated from Russian by Sonja Swenson-Khalchenia
Translation copyright © Coinflow Limited, Cyprus
AstraArt Books is an imprint of Coinflow limited, Cyprus
Published by Coinflow Limited, Cyprus
For queries please contact: tatianaborsch@yahoo.com

ISBN: 978-9925-579-26-6 (print)
ISBN: 978-9925-579-27-3 (ebook)

Contents

2021 - Birth of a new world

Based on the events of this year, my 2020 predictions, which were published on my website and in *SWAAY* magazine, are coming true (I write this article in summer 2020). We are bearing witness to an era of change; the world is teetering on the brink, and everything we thought was permanent and unshakable has turned out not to be. What else lies ahead?

It is impossible to separate the events of 2020 and 2021. These are years of major shifts, with an effect on each country, each home, and each individual. 2020's developments will continue in 2021, and there is simply no equivalent in modern history. It's safe to say that mankind has not experienced these kinds of changes in a very long time.

Major astrological events during this period are:

The first conjunction of Saturn and Jupiter in the air element will take place in Aquarius. This extremely significant event will literally take place as 2020 becomes 2021- on December 25, 2020.

This means the dawn of the Age of Aquarius, which almost everyone has heard about.

The Age of Aquarius is very long, lasting 2,160 years. It is determined by the Earth's shift from one axis to another. This transition period from one age to another can last a long time. Many astrologists believe that it will last at least 100 years. The last 20 years have been turbulent- they were vital preparation for the adoption of new rules for a new era.

All of this means that 2020 is the last year of the outgoing Age of Pisces, and 2021 is the first year of the Age of Aquarius.

Shifting eras is always linked with global shocks, crises of civilization, and economic and cultural revolutions, as well as a new perspective on religious teachings. Even the climate usually undergoes major changes.

Summer and autumn 2020, and all of 2021, are clear indicators of that.

The second most important astrological phenomenon is conflict between Saturn and Uranus, which will continue throughout 2021.

Saturn will square Uranus several times in 2021 – we can divide them into the following periods: January-March, May-the first half of July, December 2021-January 2022.

During these periods, we can expect many problems to rear their heads. It is hard to say exactly how this will influence each individual person as part of a general prediction – everything depends on your personal data, though, generally speaking, I can say that we will see the following trends in during these periods of 2021:

I.   First of all, we can expect the economic crisis to expand in scope. Many people will lose their jobs, and companies will go bankrupt.

II. In many countries, we will see social breakdown. People will organize strikes and demonstrations, and the overarching theme will be their discontent with authorities and the current order. We will see confrontation between society and power structures.

III. In global hotspots, we may see new deployments of military force or reescalation of conflict.

IV. For individuals, problems that began in 2019 or 2020 will continue, though this time, things may worsen. Remember – a chain is only as strong as its weakest link.

V.   The climate may undergo significant changes- flooding and forest fires will cause extensive damage. Large-scale migrations will be the result. In response, governments of countries in a better position may declare states of emergency or deploy troops in order to prevent unwanted migrants from crossing their borders.

VI. This interaction between Saturn and Uranus is indicative of conflict between old and new ways of life, and a difficult, irreconcilable struggle that will be reflected in all areas of life – social, economic, and political.

Saturn carries the energy of restrictions and structure. At the same time, Uranus is the planet of unexpected, revolutionary change (as well as high tech). Conflict between the two planets leads to sharp changes in existing reality. Transitioning to a new world and a new set of rules will lead to conflict.

Interaction between Saturn and Uranus speaks to opposition to both new and old ways of living, and of the rigid, irreconcilable struggle that is reflected in every sphere of life – social, economic, and political. Most peoples' lives will undergo dramatic changes, and they will have to adapt.

Economics and Politics

Saturn will square Uranus throughout 2021, and this will raise difficult questions – it is time for out with the old, in with the new. But replacing an old system with a new one is rarely a peaceful process. That is why the struggle between old and new economic orders will be a feature of 2020 and 2021.

Former economic systems will begin to transform, right before our very eyes, and these processes will go hand in hand with trade wars, political reckoning, and in some cases, armed conflict.

As the global financial crisis further unfolds, we can expect to see a stronger China, and weakened United States. Countries in the Western financial system will suffer greatly, particularly those in the Eurozone, and American political and economic satellites.

From an astrological perspective, the American presidential elections will take place during one of the most challenging periods of 2020. By now, we are used to political scandals every four years when they occur. However, I fear that the 2020 elections will put all others to shame when it comes to political upheaval.

On Election Day and the period leading up to it, Mercury and Mars will be in retrograde, which means that there will be significant incorrect or intentionally twisted information, crowds of protesters, and this will peak the last week before the elections take place, on November 3. Retrograde planets also point toward the opposition party trying to protest the election results, which will translate into large-scale scandal.

Donald Trump may be re-elected for a second term, if Joe Biden is his only opponent. Incriminating information on Biden will come to light in late September or October 2020, when he will simultaneously battle serious health issues. Generally speaking, Biden's horoscope is much weaker than Trump's.

Whoever ends up as President of the United States will have to face a series of problems in 2021- most of all conflict among members of his inner circle.

The horoscope of the United States, which was founded on the day of its Declaration of Independence, on July 04, 1776, in Philadelphia, Pennsylvania, USA, predicts that America's economic and political might will waste away, and this may take place more quickly than we can imagine.

This crisis in the American system will lead to a drop and depreciation in the US dollar in late 2020 or the first quarter of 2021. The US chart suggests that in 2021, the dollar will be replaced as a reserve currency.

As America weakens, it will face growing confrontations with other countries. In 2021, the US will wield less influence on political and economic allies.

There may even be tides of separatism within the States themselves.

Even so, I do not think the United States is threatened by the same fate as the USSR – it is unlikely to disintegrate. But it is possible that in late 2020 or early 2021, some states will declare their desire to secede, and even take some decisive steps in that direction, but full secession is not in the cards. Nonetheless, the struggle will be very difficult for America's political elite and society as a whole.

Large-scale social protests and unrest, which we saw in 2019 and 2020 will continue in 2021, though they may become more aggressive in nature.

This does not only apply to the United States. Social activism will grow worldwide. Mottos of the Age of Aquarius are FREEDOM, EQUALITY, and BROTHERHOOD, and they will be brandished in many countries around the world. This time, the conflict will not only be over ethnic or racial issues, but also pit social classes against each other – the rich versus the poor.

During the second half of 2020, and nearly all of 2021, expect an economic crisis that will spare nearly no country around the world. Many will blame their current governments, and brutal confrontations between citizens and the authorities will follow, oppositions will become active, demonstrations will take place, and instability in some countries may go so far as to topple current regimes.

England will also be dragged into financial crisis, and according to its horoscope, the worst period countrywide is likely to begin in December 2020, and last until September 2023. Expect financial problems, changes in the Royal Family (the Queen is likely to leave the throne between December 2020 and July 2021), and also innovative changes to how the country is governed.

There are also indications that in the summer and fall of 2020, a financial crisis is likely in the Russian Federation, and it will continue into 2021.

During this period, President Putin's horoscope contains indications of a systemic crisis, financial shortages, and growing opposition movements. Any leader's horoscope is largely a reflection of the state of his or her country.

Money

All countries will lean more strongly toward virtual currencies and cryptocurrencies, which will be accepted by many countries' governments over the next three to five years. This will make it easier to control cash flow, and with it, all of us.

Our reality will increasingly take place virtually, and professionals in this arena will make up the most sought-after and highly-paid class of workers.

As far as personal finance, the Zodiac sign horoscopes included in my book, "Complete Horoscope 2021" offer more specific information. But generally speaking, during a transition period, it is better to refrain from taking risks, and best to avoid investing your money in get-rich-quick schemes.

What's more, there is a saying "Don't risk your house on a sure thing"- now, that is surprisingly relevant.

Personal life

A crisis is a crisis, but love is an eternal concept. So long as humans exist, they will live and love. 2021 will likely also be a year of major changes in this arena. While tragedy will befall some, others will find happiness.

Unstable partnerships are likely to fall apart, and all the problems faced by unhappy couples are likely to rear their ugly heads.

Unexpected breakups are a possibility, and in many cases, this will be related to an existential crisis, internal discomfort, or maybe even material losses.

Couples with a sincere bond and real affection for one another may be able to take their relationship to the next level, for example, they may begin living together, or get married.

The political, economic, and social shifts underway might force many to move, find a new place to live, or acquire real estate. Many people may also find themselves immersed in issues related to housing- buying or restoring a home, and in some cases, that may be related to moving to another city or even abroad.

In that scenario, be careful and pay attention- due to the conflict between Saturn and Uranus, it is not worth making any investments in a completed construction or second home unless the project has already been proven.

People will begin to seriously reconsider their views on the concept of marriage in the near future. During the Age of Aquarius, bonds between people will be built on ideas of equality and spiritual unity.

The current trend of increasing numbers of non-traditional relationships will only grow stronger.

Differences between the sexes will gradually fade away, as Aquarius is the sign of unisex. Marriage itself will begin to resemble the classic model less and less, as it becomes free, and in some cases, "open". This may bring both advantages and serious disadvantages. Obviously, freedom is a good thing. But that freedom often goes hand in hand with loneliness.

Conflict between Saturn and Uranus will lead to a generational conflict. Saturn represents the older generation, parents, while Uranus represents rebellious children. That means that the younger generation will actively push back against pressure from their elders, and the older generation will need to become wiser and more flexible.

Health

Technology will play a greater role in medicine, affecting every branch of it.

The union of Saturn and Jupiter, and their tension toward Uranus suggest unexpected deaths, which may be due to various types of accidents and cataclysms.

Those suffering from chronic cardiovascular or spinal diseases should take special precautions.

We may encounter a "second wave" of coronavirus, or outbreaks of new, unknown diseases.

I entitled this article "Birth of a New World". Birth is a painful process, and a mother's body undergoes significant changes, but the fact remains that birth is a great joy for parents and loved ones. The same can be said for 2021. It will not be an easy year, and many will have a difficult time – whether they face problems at work or in their personal life, but that is the logical continuation of the period we live in. We will gain experience and knowledge, and see the emergence of new technology, which will open a new chapter in human history. I am certain that after a transition period, the Age of Aquarius will be the beginning of a new, wonderful world.

Tatiana Borsch

July 12, 2020

2021 Overview for all Zodiac signs

Aries

Things are steadily charging ahead in 2021, and that's for the best, especially for you. The way to the top becomes more difficult, but as they say, "no pain, no gain"!

Work. Without a doubt, the last three years have been kind to you. You've grown at work and are making more money. But 2021 will throw you a curveball, and you'll have to adapt and learn to go with the flow.

No, you're not going to change who you are, and your growing business is going to continue, one way or another. But over the course of the year, you will find yourself grappling with challenging, thorny issues with those from your inner circle, close friends, or your superiors.

This will most likely be with regard to money or other valuable property, and initially, the problem may seem hopeless. You're going to have to come back to it more than once throughout the year. Alternatively, people who have helped you or given favors in the past will be unable to do so in 2021, and you will find yourself handling a lot of problems on your own.

You'll only start to see clear progress in December, but in 2022, things will be looking much brighter – all the difficult, contentious issues will have been resolved one way or another.

The eclipses of 2021 will fall on the part of your sky responsible for relationships in general, and specifically, relationships with faraway places. That means that contacts with colleagues in other cities or abroad will become important. You will see the birth of a full partnership which has the power to totally change both your business and your life.

In some cases, a developing business or new job will make you consider moving to distant places.

New people, new friends, and new partners will appear on your horizon in 2021. This will keep things interesting, and life will keep moving forward, merrily and quickly.

Money. When it comes to finances, 2021 might bring both failure and success. The stars recommend paying closer attention to your surroundings, old friends, loved ones, and people with whom you share a common material interest. One of them may cause you to lose a lot of money from time to time.

At the same time, new sources of income may appear, so despite the problems, you will be able to maintain financial balance.

Love and family. This year, your personal life is not going to be easy. Many families will see problems involving children. This highly sensitive area of your life will require special attention. It is possible that throughout the year, a large part of your family's budget will end up going toward your children's needs.

Relationships with your relatives will become very important. In all challenging situations this year, you will be able to find support from your closest family members.

2021 will be a difficult year for those in romantic partnership. Their relationships will constantly be put to the test, and the main topic of potential issues, unfortunately, will be money or other material concerns. It's a bad thing when love and money are tied up together, and even worse when that causes problems. Remember that love plays by strict rules, and the more you demand, the less you get. If you follow that, you'll be able to mitigate any situation and come out unscathed.

Health. 2021 finds you bounding with energy, and that will help you deal with issues at work and in your personal life.

Taurus

"How steel was tempered" is your motto for 2021. You'll have to adapt to an ever-changing world, overcome obstacles, and work tirelessly to meet your goals, but it will all pay off in the end!

Work. A new cycle will begin in your life at work in 2021. It may the determine the course of events for many years to come. That opens new doors for you, which will be bizarrely intertwined with old problems.

Employees will find opportunities for a new job, and it will most likely involve more authority, either in the same place, or in a new, more promising position.

Entrepreneurs will launch new projects, using what they have done previously to their advantage. However, this may lead to confrontation with management or the powers that be.

This situation may last all year, and the stars strongly encourage everyone under your sign to be more flexible and diplomatic. But if things come to a stalemate, it would be best to bring some friends or high-level supporters to the negotiating table - there will definitely be opportunities there.

Relationships with colleagues in other cities or abroad will develop with varying success, however, you have now overcome many of the problems that troubled you in the past, and you can say the same about any past legal issues.

Money. Overall, your finances are stable, and many Taureans will see a slight increase in income this year. Expenses will drop, and that favorable trend will continue in the future.

Love and family. Your personal life may seem bumpy and restless.

Married couples on the rocks will be closer to ever to separation and divorce. Longing for something new, and possibly a different, more exciting relationship will drive many Taureans to completely change their lives. But in some cases, that process will be painful for your ex.

On the other hand, your constantly being busy at work might cause tension within your family life, so tread very lightly and let your loved ones know why you've been so absent. The same goes for couples, whether or not they are married.

Relationships with relatives that were rocky in 2020 have calmed down somewhat, and you might find yourself reconnecting with family in other cities or abroad.

Health. Despite the fact that you are going through a turbulent, tiresome, and very emotional year, you are in good health. Nonetheless, throughout the year, particularly in January, February, and December, there is a high likelihood of experiencing some kind of injury and various extreme situations. Take precautions if you can, if your job carries some kind of risk. It is recommended that all Taureans avoid situations fraught with complications.

Gemini

2021 looks like an obstacle course. On one hand, new opportunities are on the horizon. On the other, new problems are starting to crop up. In any case, there is no way back- there is nowhere to go but forward!

Work. Throughout the year, solar and lunar eclipses will take place both in your sign and your opposite sign. This means everything is in flux, and no area of your life will be left behind.

You will begin seeing new professional opportunities, and in some cases, they will involve moving or developing ties with partners from different cities or abroad. This may mean reconnecting with former associates, but under a new partnership and with a new, more promising foundation.

At the same time, unexpected problems may prevent you from moving full-speed ahead, which will hinder progress somewhat. This may be due to *force majeure,* or possibly, the erratic behavior of colleagues located abroad or in other cities.

Other challenges are likely to stem from a difficult international situation, and are likely to disrupt your plans and work.

Entrepreneurs and management should prepare for audits, which are highly likely during the second half of January, in February, June, and December. During these periods, new legal problems may arise or old ones may rear their heads again.

Things aren't perfect, but despite that, you are steadily moving ahead, and that will start to pay off closer to the end of the year.

Entrepreneurs will break new ground and find a more stable income, while employees can count on new work. Negotiations on this may start as early as Autumn 2021, and things will be in full swing by 2022.

Money. Finances may be uneven in 2021. You still aren't seeing any large income, but your expenses are reasonable and predictable.

Love and family. This year's eclipses will have a major impact on your personal life. This may mean several gripping scenarios.

Single people may meet someone interesting, and love may grow to the point where it's time to start seriously thinking about the future.

After thinking things over, many will be ready to say, "I do" and march straight down the aisle.

Less decisive Geminis might simply move in and begin living together.

However, the eclipses will force many to totally reconsider their current relationships, especially if there have been problems for years. In that case, many spouses and couples will ask themselves, "is it worth staying? Is this the right person for me?" Often, the answer will be "no".

Relationships with family members may become challenging from time to time, and more often than not, this will involve your better half's relatives, rather than your own. This may stem from intrigue, unexpected and damaging information about you, rumors, and gossip. Should this happen, the stars recommend solving the problem calmly, and avoiding conflict whenever possible.

Health. Throughout 2021, your energy levels will remain high enough and you will have no reason to fear getting sick. However, the stars strongly encourage you to be more careful when traveling, and behind the wheel. Critical months in 2021 are the second half of January, February, the second half of May, June, and December. You will find further details in the monthly predictions.

Cancer

For you, 2021 may be the year of tying up loose ends, and also building bridges toward the future. The time has come to take care of unfinished Work. It's not the most fun thing to do, but it's absolutely necessary!

Work. For many Cancers, 2021 will be a challenging year. It is a peculiar transition period, during which you'll find yourself grappling with problems from past years, repaying debts, and fulfilling various responsibilities.

Entrepreneurs and managers at every level may end up in yet another conflict with a superior, and this time, things look complicated.

Serious money or other financial obligations are at play, and you stand to lose a lot. Or you may be facing conflicts with friends or a group of like-minded people.

Legal problems from the past may also crop up again, and it's unlikely to turn out in your favor. That is why you need to try to find a reasonable compromise. You will have many opportunities to do so throughout the year.

At the same time, new opportunities for a different, more positive future, will gradually appear on the horizon. In some cases, they will be related to another city or country.

Employees may leave their place of work for various reasons, though the search for a new place for your talents is likely to drag out, so think long and hard before cutting the cord.

Money. Financially speaking, 2021 is bound to be a very difficult year. You will feel like you are bleeding money, and it may be due to unresolved issues at work, or over problems in your personal life.

In any case, remember that no financial risk is justified right now; you may not gain anything from it, and you have a lot to lose. Be particularly wary if you work in finance in any capacity – bankers, brokers, or accountants.

Love and family. In 2021, your personal life also leaves a lot to be desired. Divorced and divorcing couples may have explosive fights over property, and in some cases, drag children into the situation.

You have little chance of winning, so look for potential compromises-this is your best option right now.

Romantic relationships will start to crumble, in some cases over different outlooks on life and value systems, and in the worst cases, over money and financial issues. In this scenario, the relationship will fall apart entirely, and anyone who wants to stay together needs to take that into consideration.

Together, couples in a stable relationship can solve any problems, of which there will be many in 2021.

Health. This inauspicious year may bring a series of health-related problems. The weak and elderly need to be especially careful. It is highly likely that old and chronic wounds will be exacerbated this year. Many Cancers will find themselves taking care of a loved one's health this year, so look at all your options and take any necessary measures.

Leo

You are moving toward the end of a cycle at work, and that is why you're in for another bumpy year. You once had a clear picture of everything, but some of your goals were so difficult to reach, that you are now asking yourself whether it is worth finishing what you started. Only you can answer that question.

Work. You may become heavily dependent on your business partners. That is not always a bad thing, but this is not one of those times.

Entrepreneurs will suddenly discover that their views are radically different than those of their associates, and this will lead to conflict. In some cases, the business will fall apart.

Employees will face stiff competition in 2021. There may be unexpected conflict with their superiors, which will make them question whether they wish to continue working in that organization.

This situation may continue to ebb and flow all year, and in the most difficult situations, the stars recommend turning to friends or your mentors for help.

They are unlikely to be able to fully resolve the problem, but with some effort, they may be able to mitigate it to a degree.

The most difficult months at work may be the second half of January, February, May, and December. Closer to the end of the year, you will have some difficult decisions to make- should you continue what you started? In many cases, the answer will be no.

Money. Financially, things may look unbalanced this year, due to the mounting problems you will have to face.

Things will only improve in 2022, and you'll just have to get through 2021. In any case, you won't end up penniless, you will keep working and you'll still be making some money.

Love and family. You will go through a significant personal renaissance, though it will look differently, depending on your situation in the past.

The eclipses this year will take place in the love sector of your sky, which means that you won't find yourself alone. Single people will find a chance to start something interesting, and it might just be with someone you've known for a long time. Your relationship will move to the next level, based on love and understanding.

For spouses with grudges, their relationship will be different. Things will look tense and critical, so be careful and tread lightly, if you wish to remain together.

Alternatively, a loved one may have a problem, and you will face the difficult task of shouldering their responsibility.

Health. This year, your energy is lagging, though you won't need to worry about getting sick, as long as you follow a daily routine and remember to rest.

The elderly, weak and those suffering from cardiovascular diseases need to be particularly careful and not forget to take any preventive measures.

Virgo

"The early bird gets the worm," is your motto all year long in 2021. And you're enjoying it!

Work. 2021 may be a turning point for you at work, and when it comes to your boldest professional aspirations. The solar and lunar eclipses will take place high in your sky and call on you to march ahead.

You'll be busy with work, and things are progressing, but as they say, "every rose has its thorn." Relationships with associates in other cities or abroad may become your biggest problem this year, and the reasons for this conflict are many- these include challenges on the global stage, colleagues' unwillingness to meet you, or even the laws of another country.

Entrepreneurs will run into this at the start of the year, in January and February, and later on, as well. Are these problems that can be solved? Of course! You have been "between a rock and a hard place" for quite some time now, and you're not used to giving up. This time is no different- slowly, but surely, you will break down barriers, and remember: "a journey of a thousand miles starts with a single step".

Any legal issues will also be resolved.

In all of the most complex situations that come up this year, you'll be able to count on yourself, on old and loyal friends, as well as family members.

Employees may find themselves facing additional responsibilities, which will be rewarded handsomely. You may see a small promotion within your employer's organization.

Money. Financially, 2021 might turn out to be better than 2020 was. You'll have more money, but you'll have to work hard for it. That means earning every penny you have from honest work, because unfortunately, there are no gifts.

Love and family. Work will be so busy in 2021, that your personal life may get pushed to the back burner.

In the best-case scenario, you can expect romance with someone who is somehow linked to your job, and August and September are the most promising months for that. You may even meet someone while traveling.

Married couples will not be particularly happy this year, but they also will not face any sadness, though things may get worse for couples who are already on the rocks.

Your relationship with family members leaves much to be desired, but most likely this is the case with your in-laws, rather than your own relatives. There may be arguments, or you may end up having to help relatives in distress.

Health. If anything can interfere with your work, it is your health. Throughout the year, you are feeling a little sluggish, so a healthy lifestyle is absolutely necessary.

Take special care if you are elderly, or if you suffer from various chronic conditions. They may exacerbate and cause problems for you.

Those suffering from cardiovascular, spinal, and hormonal conditions are under particular pressure from the heavens.

Libra

2021 will bring you a glorious creative drive and new ideas, but you're going to have to work to make them a reality. You'll have to sacrifice to see the results you want, but astrologers predict you will make it happen - like you always do.

Work. From time to time, there are periods where everything about your work must change. At first, there's chaos, and then confusion - change's two constant companions.

It's possible you'll find yourself dealing with these issues in the coming year. Rarely are dreams and reality good friends, but this time you'll have to combine the two.

Your biggest problem in 2021 is money! Money is a limitation that both entrepreneurs and managers of all stripes will have to deal with. If, at the beginning of the year- January and February- you find yourself having to pay what you consider to be a large sum of money, remember that this is not the last time. Your growing business is going to require a lot of resources throughout the year, so give your ideas a reality check, and run the numbers through to the end.

Throughout 2021, the eclipses will accentuate your relationship with colleagues from other cities or abroad. There are several possible outcomes - some progress may be made, but you're going to have to work hard at it. Late May, June, and December are likely to be major, difficult periods for you in this regard.

During these periods, keep a close eye on your own interests, and remember that a compromise can only be mutually beneficial - too many concessions on your end will lead to setbacks in the future.

What's more - as in the past, entrepreneurs and managers need to be more attentive to their subordinates, as not all of them are honest, reliable, and competent. If you are thinking of replacing someone, that is the right decision.

Those with legal problems will have to make a choice – freedom or money, and in most cases, the former will win out.

Money. 2021 may turn out to be devastating, financially speaking. In some cases, it will be due to business, in others, your personal life, such as family or children's needs. You'll make up for it in 2022, so it's not worth worrying over.

Love and family. Your personal life will certainly be interesting this year, but it will also be restless. Many families will face problems involving their children, you might even say that the younger generation is staging a mutiny. In some cases, it will be costly – you'll have to periodically use large amounts of your family budget paying for children's needs.

Many will start building something serious – it might be a family business, or rebuilding a home. You might also buy a home or summer house. In either case, it will cost you money.

Expect a bumpy year if you're partnered up. Things will be stable and reliable, but you're also in for outbursts of jealousy, all kinds of disagreements, and financial problems, too.

Things will settle down near the end of the year, and in many cases, couples will decide to get married or move in together. Some families will see new babies or grandchildren born.

Health. You're healthy, energetic, and very attractive in 2021, and everyone who crosses your path will notice.

Scorpio

One chapter of your life has ended. You have a new path ahead, but no one said it would be a straight one. In any case, there's no going back, and for some that will be related to work, for others, due to their romantic or family life.

Work. Many Scorpios will see major events in their personal lives this year. If your interests are mainly work-related, get ready for some surprises.

Entrepreneurs and managers may end up seeing conflict with business associates, and land, real estate, or other large properties may be at stake. Storms will flare up and quiet down, but you won't see a compromise solution until December 2021, or maybe even January-February 2022.

During the first half of the year, employees may find themselves facing stiff competition, and during the second half, major changes will be underway in their organization. It is highly likely that you will see leadership changes.

Those planning to open a business in another city or abroad may spend a lot of time dealing with organizational issues, which might be accompanied by further problems. This won't hinder your progress, but it will take up time from your schedule.

All this means you won't be bored, so buckle up and remember - experience counts.

The most difficult periods of 2021 are the second half of January, February, the second half of May, June, December.

Money. You'll likely be dealing with money problems throughout the year. It may be related to inconsistency at work, or your personal life.

Love and family. Many Scorpios may see major events at home and involving their family in 2021.

Those facing trouble in their marriages might find themselves arguing frequently, and in the worst cases, opt for separation or divorce.

If this describes you, keep in mind that the natural consequence of all this may be a struggle over property or real estate.

Even when couples are getting along, they are likely to face problems with their home, apartment, or other real estate, but in this case, you are facing unscrupulous opponents, who may be developers, or crooks of all stripes.

Children bring you joy, and closer to the end of the year, and when it comes to them, expect a wonderful streak, in some cases, they will bring quarreling parents together.

Scorpios who are used to wearing multiple hats are going to have to make some ultimate decisions, as it won't be possible to juggle everything in 2021.

Those moving somewhere faraway may have difficulties solving matters related to improving their lives.

Health. In 2021, you're feeling sluggish, and be very cautious if you are elderly or suffer from a chronic condition. Young and healthy Scorpios should watch their weight, remember to get some exercise, and eat a balanced diet.

Sagittarius

New opportunities await in 2021, and they will without a doubt go hand in hand with new challenges of fate. But you won't have time to get used to it - after spending a long time stuck between a rock and a hard place, you're steadily moving ahead.

Work. In 2021, the most restless Sagittarians will find themselves working one way or another with other cities or countries. Entrepreneurs are expanding their activities and dealing with colleagues from afar. But plans are only half the battle, and actually carrying them out may bring you face to face with strong opposition from various circumstances. It may involve the laws of another country, or discrepancies between your professional foundation and far-reaching plans and wide-scale activities.

Entrepreneurs will have to deal with their subordinates in order to restore some sense of order. Surprisingly, this will be a long and rocky road. People who you'd expect to give you their utmost support and assistance might be playing their own games. Keep in mind that by taking measures in advance, and constantly keeping an eye on things, you'll be able to avoid disaster once things become critical.

Employees can expect problems with their team, or outright hostility from a colleague.

The most difficult periods in 2021 will be the second half of January, February, the second half of May, June, and December.

Despite some hiccups, you'll be able to reach some of the goals you set for yourself, and in 2022, you'll see it wasn't all for nothing.

Money. Your financial situation will be no different in 2021 when it comes to stability. Money will come and go, but that is the working process. The most promising months, as far as material concerns go, are January, March, April, May, the second half of August, September, and the second half of December.

Love and family. 2021 is a time for major changes in your personal life. Many will be planning a move, and will be carrying out their life plans during different periods of the year. In many cases, these are challenging events, which will go hand in hand with various setbacks, and the difficult international situation or laws from another country are most likely among them.

For many reasons, many Sagittarians will face various problems with their relatives. It may be that a family member will have a grudge against you. Or perhaps you will find yourself supporting family facing difficult circumstances.

The eclipses this year will take place in your sign, as well as in your opposite sign, which will drive those who are dissatisfied with their family situation or love life to reconsider the relationship. In the most extreme cases, this may lead to truly ending the relationship, but in others, simply a temporary separation.

Thanks to the eclipses, single people may meet someone interesting and build a lasting relationship.

Health. You are rather energetic this year, but the stars strongly recommend paying more attention while traveling or behind the wheel.

Capricorn

The last few years have been a bit of a rush for you at work. You did a lot, but as one chapter comes to a close, another one opens. As before, your protector Saturn is guiding you both forward and upward.

Work. Major changes are not predicted at work, and revolution is not on the horizon. However, Jupiter is shifting to the sector of the sky responsible for moves, changes, and you're suddenly feeling like you can't sit still.

Slowly but surely, entrepreneurs are seeing their plans come to fruition, and this is related to growing your business in faraway places. For now, though, they are just plans, and translating them into action won't be possible until 2022.

The most persistent Capricorns will begin negotiations on this in late

May, June, and July, as well as December.

Employees will also strengthen their position at work. Things keep moving ahead, and your money is growing.

Money. Despite the obvious benefits at work, and a higher income, you can't say things are totally calm when it comes to the material area of your life. It isn't necessarily due to a lack of income, but growing demands from your loved ones, especially children.

Love and family. Your personal life is not particularly stable in 2021. Even happily married Capricorns might argue frequently and annoy each other more often.

Problems with children will complete the picture. Maybe they will be rebellious, misbehave, stage a real mutiny. While in some cases, this is a natural part of growing up, that is unlikely to be true most of the time. Throughout 2021, you'll find yourself spending a hefty amount of money on your children's needs, and the stars strongly urge you to separate actual needs from capriciousness - but only you can make that happen.

For most Capricorns in a relationship, 2021 will be a real test of strength. Uranus - the planet of surprises and the unexpected - is holding firmly to the love sector of your sky, and this time, the surprises may not be so pleasant.

Perhaps your partner will act out in ways you didn't expect, that is, making moral or material complaints. On the other hand, you yourself may be making a decision to develop the relationship, and this will be a difficult step in every direction.

Health. In 2021, your energy is rather low, and you may be experiencing mood swings, linked to the various facets of your life colliding. The stars recommend that you live a healthy lifestyle all year long, and learn to take a step back and look at problems from above. That will keep you strong in body and spirit.

You may have to take care of a family member's health in the coming year, which you will do, sparing no effort.

Aquarius

All year, Jupiter and Saturn will be in your sign, and that means your time has come! A new life cycle is beginning, and it will be very successful!

Work. The coming year will open new doors for you professionally. Say goodbye to projects that change at the last minute, dealing with office intrigue, and other conflicts at work. You're becoming more confident, and tuning into all the resources at your disposal.

Employees can be sure they will strengthen their position at work, while entrepreneurs can look forward to getting projects they've been planning for a long time off the ground.

For various reasons, everything you've had on the back burner is finally taking center stage.

Nothing is ever entirely perfect, and this time, despite the obvious successes of 2021, you will also have to deal with unexpected problems. To a greater extent, they will affect entrepreneurs, who have to deal with a number of delicate issues related to real estate. Conflicts may stretch out all year long, and at the end, turn out in your favor. Critical periods in 2021 are the second half of January, February, the end of May, June, and also December. You should react calmly to hostile attracts from your opponents, and collect the necessary paperwork, with the assistance of responsible lawyers.

Money. Your finances are improving somewhat, and that will become particularly apparent closer to the end of the year. There is no doubt that everything you do in 2021 will lead to excellent material results in the future. The main prizes will be within reach in 2022.

Love and family. While things are calm at work, this is less the case in your personal life. The 2021 eclipses will accentuate the sector of the sky related to romance and love stories, which means that many Aquarians will be thinking about an unexpected change in their marital status.

Someone you've known well and for a long time may begin exerting their rights, and in some cases, that will be in the midst of separation or divorce.

If that happens, there is no escaping the myriad of problems with joint property, and most of all, real estate.

These disputes will last all year long, and may calm down before flaring up again, with no acceptable compromise until December.

Alternatively, you may face problems with your children, which parents will have to resolve together, whether they get along or are on a crash course toward divorce.

Regardless of what they are, these issues will require you to pay attention and get involved.

Health. Throughout the year, the stars recommend that you take care of yourself and live a healthy lifestyle. Stern Saturn has settled into your sign for the next few years; it is the planet of duty, discipline, and responsibility toward everything, particularly yourself.

Pisces

2021 will be difficult for you. You will have to adapt to circumstances that are constantly in flux, and show agility as you maneuver between the hot and cold currents surrounding you on all sides. You will not disappoint, and near the end of the year, you will be able to celebrate your victory.

Work. For most entrepreneurs and managers, 2021 will be a test of strength. Those dealing with longstanding legal problems may find themselves facing unexpected twists and turns. New claims, various audits, and visits from regulatory bodies are highly likely.

Otherwise, you may face problems with your colleagues from other cities or abroad, who may shift their intentions. The best outcome is that they throw a wrench in your joint projects, and in the worst-case scenario, they end things entirely. Alternatively, challenges on the international stage may be at fault.

Employees will face problems with coworkers, and may think about finding a better place for their talents. These opportunities are there, but not in 2021. You will have to wait until 2022.

Your first steps in negotiations on this matter are not likely to start until December 2021- keep that in mind, if you feel an urge to cut and run. Remember that in 2021, those around you will zero in on your weaknesses rather than your strengths, and therefore, keep a close eye on everything you do and say.

Critical months this year are the second half of January, February, the end of May, June, and December. By the end of December, when Jupiter enters your sign, you will be able to safely say that you have made your way to the end of the tunnel - somewhat bruised and battered, but with your head held high!

Money. Things are a bit conflicting when it comes to finances this year, though when times get tough, you can always turn to an old friend or loved one for help. They can help you with professional matters, as well as emerging financial difficulties.

Love and family. Things may be different in your personal life. Those who have been partnered up for some time will be making decisions on marriage or living together, and will certainly buy a place to live.

Pisces who quit their jobs may do so due to pregnancy or marriage.

In many families, there will be problems with relatives, though it is impossible to describe in the general forecast each particular case. There may be serious arguments, or you may find yourself involved in your close relatives' problems.

With all the problems you are facing in 2021, you will be able to count on those closest to you - your spouse or other loved ones.

Romantic Pisces and those who are sitting on the fence should keep in mind that 2021 is the year things will be brought into the light, and act accordingly.

Health. Those who are spared problems at work and at home may find themselves dealing with health issues. It is likely old chronic illnesses will exacerbate, and unexpected appearance of new issues is a strong possibility, so take care of yourself and be observant.

Throughout the year, be careful when traveling or driving - accidents and emergencies are extremely likely in 2021. If your family is expecting a child, only select medical facilities which you trust 100%!

January

Aries

"Business before pleasure!" This will be your motto throughout January. And the stars will help you!

Work. January is a time of buzzing activity and overcoming various obstacles. It is a tense, but overall positive time, when you will be able to tackle problems from the past, while also outlining your plans for the future.

Many Aries will have an excellent chance to prove themselves as leaders, able to inspire others and organize them well.

Employees will fall into their bosses' favor, and entrepreneurs will see that promising projects are being promoted.

Still, you wouldn't describe January as "calm". "A fly in the ointment in a barrel of honey" may describe a relationship with an old friend, like-minded people, or influential mentors. It will be over finances, as suddenly, due to the strange position of people you were previously able to trust, and this time, you have a lot to lose. The situation will escalate near the middle of the month, and will continue in the future. Moving forward, the next "D-Day" looks like it will be in late February.

Relationships with associates in other cities or countries will develop with varying success - some things will turn out, and with others you will still have work left to do. But this is a story you've seen before, and you've always managed. You'll do it again.

Money. Financially, January is a bit of a conundrum. On one hand, you won't find yourself without money, but on the other, large, unplanned expenses or unexpected losses are likely. In any case, stay away from financial risks, sign any necessary papers in advance, don't make any promises related to money or other material values – following through will not come easily.

Love and family. You are immersed in your work this month, and your personal life may end up on the back burner. And this is the best-case scenario. In the worst case, many Aries will experience turbulence and find themselves constantly arguing with those closest to them. This may be over different worldviews and unresolved financial issues.

If this sounds like you, the stars suggest fastening your seatbelts and exercising patience. If you let it all go, these problems may only snowball and lead to serious arguments next month.

It's also possible that a loved one will experience problems, and you will have to help them – with words, deeds, and money.

Health. All month, you are healthy, energetic, and enthusiastic. But don't overdo it physically. You run a risk of exhausting yourself and suddenly being injured. The 12th through 28th of January is the most inauspicious time for this.

Taurus

You want freedom, but breaking out on your own is hard, right now. The stars recommend taking a long, hard look at the situation, and accepting what you cannot change, and waiting for better times! They are sure to come!

Work. January will bring a lot of ups and downs at work. Many Taureans will have plans in other cities or abroad, and put all their efforts into reaching that cherished goal. You will be able to make some progress in that regard – at the very beginning of the month, you might take a trip that proves to be successful. Otherwise, you may begin constructive negotiations with colleagues from far away.

In mid-January, stormy clouds loom on the horizon. During that time, employees are likely to experience problems with management, and entrepreneurs will face trouble with the powers that be.

The stars recommend watching your behavior when dealing with all authorities: regulatory bodies, members of law enforcement, tax authorities, even if you just want to get rid of them. You must always keep your eyes open with these individuals, especially now. Be patient, and remember, what happens in mid-January may be just a preview of hard times to come.

Money. January is likely to be a neutral month for your finances. There aren't many expenses, but your income isn't particularly high, either. The largest sums of money may come in from January 23 to 25.

Love and family. During the first half of the month, your personal life is uneventful. There is a possibility of starting a passionate relationship with someone living in another city or abroad, and going on an exciting trip with a loved one.

However, the second half of the month will not be successful – and it's all on you! Many Taureans, particularly those born from April 21 to May 2, will be in a strange, almost revolutionary mood; they will be abrupt and want to do everything their own way. Their relationship has never seen this before, and now these qualities may make things unpleasant for you and your loved ones. Arguments are not your forte, so try to be flexible, and if you have any disagreements, seek an acceptable compromise, even if sometimes that is a hard thing to do.

Many Taureans will come to serious disagreements with their parents, and in some cases, it will lead to huge feuds. If you have any shared business, the situation will become even more complicated.

Health. Throughout January, you will be feeling great, and your energy may be through the roof. Be sure to use it only for peaceful ends, and avoid conflict with others, unless it is absolutely necessary. This month, your motto is "measure twice and cut once". If you let that guide you, you will master the most challenging games of chess.

Gemini

This month, you'll need a thoughtful plan, down to the last detail. And keep every possible outcome in mind, without focusing too much on the most pleasant. This way, you'll avoid mistakes, or at least minimize them.

Work. The first half of the month will be calm and predictable. Many will be doing business at home, and that includes methodical, organizational tasks. The second half of the month will be turbulent and chaotic. Several problems will emerge involving associates from other cities or abroad, which will be directly reflected in your working processes. You may have to grapple with an unusual situation, or unpleasant secrets from those around you.

Entrepreneurs and managers at every level may find themselves the target of various auditing authorities, including those from international bodies. If that is your case, keep in mind that things are unlikely to be resolved in January; they will get much more difficult next month.

A planned move or business launch in another city or country will be challenging, and as a result, things will stall or end up on the verge of collapse. In that case, keep a cool head as you deal with the problems, and be patient – time heals all wounds, and this way you will be able to carry out everything you planned and dreamed.

Travel planned for the second half of January may not happen or may turn out to be less-than-successful.

Money. January is likely to be neutral, financially speaking. In the first month, expect support from your spouse, parents, or loved ones. During the second half of the month, you can be assured of major expenses, mostly related to solving the problems that will arise.

Love and family. Expect additional difficulties in your personal life this month.

In the first half of January, family life may be calm, but during the second half, you are likely to face problems with family – not your own relatives, but those of your spouse or partner. Perhaps arguments will be likely – family members will face unexpected problems, and you will have to help them, in both word and deed.

Many Geminis will be very busy trying to improve their lives, and this may mean carrying out various repairs, or acquiring items to make everyday life easier or more beautiful.

Health. You are feeling sluggish in January, but not to the point of being seriously ill.

The main danger this month is travel! From January 11 to February 20, be careful and pay attention! Accidents, injuries, and unpleasant incidents behind the wheel are highly likely during this period. Additionally, unless it is absolutely essential, it is better to avoid taking any trips, and that goes for travel for both business or pleasure.

Cancer

In January, you will have to ask yourself – do you have enough strength to continue the fight? Do you have enough resources? And most importantly – "is it worth it?"

Work. During the first half of January, you might draw a friend or mentor in a high position to your business. Everything will start out fine – you can count on both the moral and more tangible, material support. But once you start discussing the details, be attentive, and discuss the terms of cooperation in advance. By the second half of the month, it will be clear that the services you were counting on may turn out to come at too high a cost, and not quite live up to expectations.

Alternatively, for various reasons, those you previously counted on will be unable to provide you with their usual support, and you will have to find your way on your own. Accept that this situation is going to continue, and not resolve itself overnight. That goes for Cancers with previous legal issues, and those still grappling with painful matters from the summer of 2020.

Money. Your finances are causing you problems. You're bleeding money in January, and that will not end until February. The stars recommend all Cancers keep tabs on their money and avoid any hasty spending.

Be particularly vigilant if your work is directly linked to finances – if you are a broker, banker, accountant, or have another position responsible for money. January brings with it losses, rather than any profits.

Love and family. January promises a series of unpleasant surprises when it comes to your personal life. This applies most to couples whose relationship has been at a stalemate, whether recently or for quite some time. They will fight over money, property, and there are no winners here. Everything that can go wrong will, so seek compromise, early on if you can.

Believe the stars – you are in a vulnerable position, and peace is more beneficial to you than war. And don't count on any support – when things are most critical, no one will be able to help you.

Spouses in a stable relationship will be able to overcome any challenges, as long as they turn to wisdom and love.

Health. Health issues may beset those who have been mercifully spared professional or personal woes. Unexpected illnesses are highly likely this month, so avoid situations involving any risk, and be very careful with any sharp objects.

The second half of the month will be challenging in every way, when unexpected incidents will be highly likely.

The elderly or weak should be particularly careful – this month it is likely that old, chronic illnesses will resurface, and new ones will appear.

Leo

January will have you making difficult, but potentially life-altering decisions. This involves people you counted on. There are no friends, now – only business, and nothing more!

Work. You've worked hard and are right to expect that your services are respected and appreciated. Right now, you're busy and things are progressing. Though the first half of January promises calm waters, the second half will bring storms involving your associates. You may be driven apart by different visions of how your work should look now or in the future, and who is in charge. As things course forward, you might say that your position is vulnerable, and you'll end up having to give in.

Don't let things boil over into open conflict or confrontation, which is the clear trend. Sit down, negotiate, try to find a workable way to cooperate, and remember that even the worst peace is better than a good fight – especially now.

During the second half of January, employees may see their relationships with management grow complicated, and this may include stiff competition and various types of intrigue. Moving forward, you can predict that problems that begin now will exacerbate in the future, so prepare to defend yourself. Learn to be patient and document everything, if you can.

Money. Though you are putting out fires at work, your money is still coming in. It may be regular, and the largest sums will arrive closer to the end of the month- January 30, 31.

Love and family. Your personal life is going through an interesting, but very difficult period. Single people can expect someone from their past to reappear, and your relationship with this person will require special attention.

Not everyone in your circle will approve of this relationship, particularly your relatives and parents. It is difficult to predict what the outcome will be in each case, but there is cause for concern. Do what you feel you have to, but you may periodically find yourself asking, "is this really what I want?"

Married couples in stable relationships may overcome work issues together, but you may also encounter quarrels and misunderstandings.

Another possibility – those close to you will need your support, and you will have to assist.

Health. This month, you're feeling a bit sluggish, so take care of yourself and avoid getting a cold or viral infection. Keep a healthy lifestyle, don't overeat, and be careful with alcohol. These basic precautions can go a long way in avoiding complications now and down the road.

Virgo

If you examine a problem from all angles, you are likely to find a way around it. A logical, balanced approach is your trump card, and now is the time to play it!

Work. During the first half of the month, things are quiet at work, and that is likely due to the holidays, which may be extended in your case. Things will really pick up the second half of January, and a number of problems will become unavoidable.

Relationships with your colleagues from other cities or abroad will unexpectedly become complicated, which will throw a wrench in your work processes and cast doubt on many plans.

Alternatively, legal problems loom on the horizon, and they may be serious. However, events over the last few years have calmed you down, so don't get discouraged or panic, slowly but surely, you will manage. Remind yourself frequently that "there are no problems that can't be solved," and as the Bible says, "God only gives us what we can handle." You need a long-term plan, because there is no quick fix to the kind of problems you are facing.

Money. Your financial situation is likely to be neutral in January. You don't have many expenses, but your income isn't high, either. Dates you can expect to receive the largest sum of money are January 5, 6, 14, 15, 23-25.

Love and family. Everything is just fine in your personal life. During the first half of January, you might take a trip, or get a change of scenery that will have a positive impact on your current relationships. You are loved, taken care of, inspiring – what else could you want? Moreover, the moment any clouds appear on your horizon at work, your loved ones give you the support you need. Children are delighted, during the first half of January, they will spend many happy moments with their parents.

Despite the positive outlook, the stars still do not recommend delegating too much responsibility to your loved ones. You have enough energy and strength to handle things on your own.

Health. During the first half of January, your energy levels are high enough, and you have no reason to fear illnesses. But during the second half of the month, you will go through a difficult period, when your body will experience a series of shocks.

The stars suggest avoiding bad habits, and living a healthy lifestyle, as well as getting regular exercise. From January 17 to 20, be very careful when traveling or driving – there is a high likelihood of accidents and unfortunate incidents on the road during this period!

Libra

It's worth taking care of yourself in January. You have gone through some challenging times, and that isn't all. When one problem is resolved, another one takes its place. You've been aching for some respite, and now, the time has come!

Work. Things are calm at work in January. But pay attention to financial matters, and don't overestimate your strength – it is not worth spreading yourself too thin and believing someone else's promises.

Your relationships with colleagues in other cities or abroad are very uneven, in some cases, things work out, in others, they don't – but this is nothing new to you.

In the past, entrepreneurs and managers dealt with delicate issues involving real estate and land. This time, however, it is about money, and various kinds of compensation and pay.

Your problems will all peak in the second half of January, right when your associates want to settle accounts. Be ready for the situation to logically continue into the next month, or maybe even longer. For that reason, don't neglect things, and take any necessary steps as soon as possible.

Money. Financially, January is a very difficult month, and it may see you losing most of your hard-earned capital. This devastating trend may be due to ups and downs at work, or perhaps stem from your personal life.

In either case, though, expect a dispute over real estate, land, and other large assets. Parents will be forced to spend large amounts on their children, their education, and development.

You'll lose some money in January, but things will not end there. Be ready to lose more in February.

Love and family. The feeling that you are swimming upstream may not leave you when it comes to your personal life. Parents might find themselves constantly arguing with their children, or spending exorbitant sums of money on them. In the worst-case scenario, you will be doing both, so take a good look at all potential outcomes and take steps as early as possible.

To single people with a weakness for adventurous romance, the stars recommend watching out for casual dating, handsome devils and *femmes fatales*, and in general be careful with your partners. The likelihood of things going up in flames is high.

If you run into people from your past, don't let your guard down – trust what they do, not what they say. The astrologer suggests that they need something from you- both moral and material support. If you aren't ready for that, don't make any hasty promises, as obligations can become an overwhelming burden, both now and later on.

Those in stable partnerships can get through this month's problems together, and in many cases, those problems will involve real estate for you or your children.

Health. This month, you are not particularly energetic, but during the second half of January, you will face many reasons for excitement, so try to keep a cool head and make sure you get enough sleep. Right now, sleep is your best medicine.

Scorpio

Try to listen more and talk less, and trust your intuition, too, in order to better analyze things. Right now, i's more important than ever!

Work. The first half of January will be totally calm. Many will take time to travel or for active negotiations with colleagues from afar.

The second half of January will not be so easy. Entrepreneurs will face serious disagreements with partners with regard to real estate. If that is your case, be careful – problems starting now are likely to continue into the next month, and you're about to begin a serious struggle with no end in sight.

With all the difficult scenarios this month, it's worth staying in touch with family – their support will be valuable and timely.

Help might also come from a colleague from another city or abroad. It is possible that they will influence hostile partners, by acting as an intermediary or attorney.

Money. You might say your financial situation in January is neutral. Disagreements with associates will not incur losses, but you will have to keep problems under control. This may involve either work or your personal life.

Love and family. In many cases, a difficult situation involving real estate will affect your personal life. Spouses who have been together for a long time may end up quarreling, and exacerbate to the point of divorce or disputes over real estate.

Stable couples will face another problem – they may have gotten involved with some sort of crook recently, or possibly a long-delayed construction project. Other machinations involving housing are also possible.

In all cases, help will come from your family members, as well as skilled and responsible attorneys.

Health. In January, you are feeling energetic and have no fear of illness.

But during the second half of the month, try to avoid conflict and dangerous situations in crowded places. You are highly likely to get wrapped up in something unpleasant with unpredictable consequences.

Also, be careful when handling sharp objects and electrical appliances.

Sagittarius

The planets are calling you to move forward, while also creating obstacles. To summarize, the most restless and rambunctious sign of the Zodiac will not be bored!

Work. During the first half of the month, things will be calm, predictable, and generally lucky. Things are moving ahead, new projects are starting, and they're bringing money with them.

But during the second half of January, you will run into some unexpected bumps in the road. Maybe your ambitious plans have not won the support of colleagues from other cities or countries, or perhaps you are dealing with problems involving a subordinate, if you are a manager or entrepreneur.

Employees are facing challenges with colleagues, and possibly intrigue or outright antagonism.

Trips planned for the second half of January may not occur, or may not be what you had in mind.

Give these issues their due attention, or they may be become more serious than they initially appear. That will become clear very quickly, next month.

Money. Financially, January is quite safe. Money will come in regularly, and the amount will grow a bit. Expect the greatest amounts on January 4, 5, 7, 8, 12, 13, 21, 22, 30, and 31.

Many Sagittarians will have to pay off debts, either their own, or even worse – someone else's.

Love and family. Your personal life is anything but boring. In many families, difficult situations involving relatives can be expected, sometimes there will be major arguments, and others, a close relative will face a difficult situation.

Moves planned to another city or abroad will be rife with unexpected problems, but it is impossible to predict how each case will turn out. Everyone will find cause for concern, so look into every possible outcome and take steps in advance. You are unlikely to resolve everything, but you can certainly mitigate it.

Trips planned for the second half of the month may not happen, so it is best to reschedule them for another time.

For those who are partnered up, this is also not an easy month. You may have various types of hurdles in your way making things complicated, and you might be facing a temporary separation.

Health. For most of the month, you are not particularly energetic, so take care of yourself and be observant. Throughout the month, especially during the second half, be attentive while traveling or driving, because the likelihood of an accident or other unfortunate incident is rather high during this time.

Capricorn

"Flexibility" is the word of the month. Think of workarounds. Attempts to get ahead will only lead to negative results, and that goes for both work and love.

Work. This month, you may not be up to working, and most likely all of your thoughts will be wrapped up in your personal life. That will be the case for everyone in the first half of January.

You will get busy at work during the second half of January, but several different issues that have been marinating for some time now may prevent you from going full speed ahead. You may find yourself disagreeing with a friend, like-minded individuals, or a superior, and, as usual, it's about money. If you are facing a similar situation, remember that it is not going away any time soon.

Your relationships with colleagues in other cities or abroad are, however, going well, and in the first half of the month you may go on a successful trip.

Money. Financially, January is not particularly promising, as you have a lot of expenses and most of them are related to your personal life. You may face financial problems involving your children, or your partner's demands.

Love and family. Many Capricorns will be immersed in personal problems this month.

Children will cause a lot of headaches for those with families; things may get out of control, and getting things back on track may take up an outsize portion of the family budget. This may go along with conflicts and emotional tests. It is likely that all this will be unexpected, but in fact, it has been a long time coming. So, collect yourself and come up with a plan of action- there is no other way out.

January is a difficult month for those in relationships. Turbulent relationships may become serious, and more than simply feelings are at play – it will revolve around money or other things of material value.

Otherwise, a loved one will need a large amount of money from you as support, and if you agree to it, it is likely that you will avoid drama. However, these problems are unlikely to end in January, they will continue next month, when things will only get worse.

Health. During the first half of the month, you are feeling energetic and in good health. But during the second half of the month, your well-being takes a turn for the worse, and things may get out of control- you are certainly not used to this. Don't let this get you down! There is always a silver lining, setbacks can teach us a lot.

Aquarius

This month, you should take care of yourself. You will experience spiritual discord, melancholy, and poor well-being might overshadow things for most Aquarians. But all things shall pass!

Work. The first half of January is likely to be calm, and not particularly exciting. You will be wrapped up in the endless holiday events. Many will be busy with family and things at home, where several problems will have unfolded.

Work will bring you back to reality during the second half of the month, and here, many Aquarians will face a series of problems. It is most likely that they will involve some kind of real estate or other large assets. An intense fight is ahead, and there is no time to dither!

Moving forward, you can say that the problems will not end in January, and will instead grow larger and continue into February. However, with some perseverance, you will pull ahead. All you have to do is keep moving and believe in yourself.

Money. Your finances are stable in January. Money will be coming in regularly, but it is unlikely that most of it will be from your usual place of employment. You might make a small profit from a real estate transaction, support from your parents, spouse, or other loved ones.

Love and family. Most Aquarians will see major events at home and with their family this month.

Often, you will have to deal with issues related to real estate, minor repairs and other changes around your home are also likely, due to unexpected needs.

Couples on the rocks will share property, especially housing. Arguments over this will begin during the first part of the month, and you can count on some unpleasant and unexpected surprises.

All the developments this month may have long-term consequences, so collect yourself and prepare to defend yourself – or perhaps get ready to go on the offensive, which may turn out to be more productive. This advice goes for all Aquarians dealing with delicate matters related to real estate.

Health. This month, you are a little sluggish, so take care of yourself, and avoid any possibility of catching a cold or infection.

Pisces

You always have to fight for what you believe in, even when it seems like you have no hope of winning. In fact, you always do have a chance, and when you need it most, that chance will appear before you, plain as day.

Work. The first half of January is a great time for you to relax and combine business with pleasure, while cultivating necessary relationships at work, and having a good time. This includes meeting up with old friends, talking to your superiors, and meeting new, interesting people.

During the second half of the month, however, things will start to look dysfunctional. You will face unexpected problems, which may look different in each individual case.

Some secrets may come to light, which might damage your reputation and cast doubt on your previous achievements.

Alternatively, you may learn something about your associates and colleagues, which will force you to reconsider the relationship and lead to serious conflict.

You will also rethink relationships with colleagues from other cities or abroad. For various reasons, things will become complicated, or break off for some time.

If any of that applies to you, remember that these issues will likely not be resolved in January; they will probably become more serious next month.

Trips planned for the second half of January will likely be unsuccessful.

Money. January is likely to be a neutral month as far as your finances are concerned. Both income and expenses will be predictable and reasonable. Problems at work will not be reflected yet in your bank account, and in any case, the biggest casualty this month will be your reputation, which may affect your relationship with business partners.

Love and family. During the second half of the month, those whose interests are more focused on their personal lives will face some challenges. The first half of January will be frenetic, fun, and interesting – there may be travel, and excitement with close friends, relatives, and loved ones. However, unexpected problems may crop up during the second half of the month, requiring you to think seriously about the future of your relationships.

Secrets will come to light – either yours or those of someone close to you. Your relationship with family members will suddenly grow complicated, and you may have serious arguments. After studying the problem at hand, you will understand that you should have done something differently, that you didn't think to do in the heat of the moment. Everything will be alright, these things happen. The most important thing is to extricate yourself from the situation. Though you might fight fire with fire at work, when it comes to your personal life, this only leads to disaster. Be flexible, diplomatic, and wise – this is your trump card, and now is the time to play it.

Health. During the first half of January, you are feeling great and have no reason to fear illness.

During the second half of the month, however, you will not be so lucky. Problems may strike right in the middle of the month. This may mean that old, chronic illnesses are returning, or that new ones are appearing. During the second half of January, there is a danger of injury and emergencies. Remember that, and try to protect yourself. Drivers should be particularly careful behind the wheel- there is a high probability of traffic accidents during this period. The stars also recommend that you refrain from travel, unless it is absolutely essential. Things will not go as planned, and you will find nothing but trouble.

February

Aries

It seems you took a dead-end road. But don't get too discouraged! There are other paths, and when you need it the most, they will become crystal clear to you.

Work. Your main concern this month will be your relationship with a friend or high-level benefactor. This will involve money or other financial obligations, and, as often happens, each party may have a different version of the events. So long as the situation is not resolved, much of your time will be spent in conflict and quarrels, and thus far, there are no winners.

This may lead to some ambiguity, and your task will be patiently getting through the most difficult periods, which will be frequent this month. You will engage in all sorts of intrigue and nuances here, so pick a strategy and don't lose your cool if things don't turn out the way you'd like.

Money. This month may turn out to be devastating. You will be dealing with large expenses all of February, so keep an eye on funds and reduce your risk of losses. Those who work in finance – bankers, accountants, and brokers – should be especially careful. There are no risks worth taking this month, and they will bring nothing but losses.

Love and family. Everything is quiet in your personal life, but only as quiet as your life is today. Nonetheless, those in relationships may find themselves growing apart, and married couples will feel friction with their children.

Couples on the rocks (both married couples and those who have not yet walked down the aisle) may start to doubt their future together, but nothing is going to happen yet this month. What's more, confrontation between Mars and Venus will force you to reconsider certain periods in your relationships, as your partner's virtues and shortcomings will come to light.

Love always hopes for the best, though, and it's not worth losing faith over a few bumps in the road.

Health. For most of February, you will be feeling rather good, and it is only as of the 27th that you will start to feel sluggish. All month long, your emotions will be up and down, so try to get enough sleep and eat properly.

Taurus

Even if things look anxious and tense, everything that happens this month will do you good. Any victory has its costs, and that is always the case.

Work. Things are interesting, but very difficult at work. More than likely, there are changes underway, and that is cause for worry and concern. Rest assured, as you get closer to March, everything will fall into place. As long as you avoid conflicts, don't force or hurry things. Let it all fall into place; as they say, there is a time and a place for everything!

Relationships with your colleagues from other cities or abroad are going well, and closer to the end of the month, you will get some good news from afar, or perhaps go on a fruitful journey.

Entrepreneurs will give a valiant effort at reestablishing themselves, while employees will try to climb the company ladder. The astrologist suggests that while businesses will eventually be successful, that will come somewhat later, rather than right away.

Money. Your money situation is stable this month; money is coming in regularly, and you can expect to receive the largest sums from February 21 to 23.

Your expenses are low, predictable, and reasonable.

Love and family. Your personal life is unlikely to give you too much trouble this month – work is taking up much of your time. Yet, despite being so busy, give your loved ones some attention, and don't be too categorical or strict, as you have a clear tendency to do.

What's more – if your work or social obligations are taking up too much of your time and your loved ones are displeased, be sure to spend time with your family on the weekends.

Those in a relationship may not see their partners as often as they would like, or they may part ways for various reasons. Whether this is temporary or permanent depends on you alone – the ball is in your court.

Health. All month, you are healthy, energetic, and ready to climb mountains. The stars strongly urge that you only use this energy for peaceful means, and everything will be fine!

Gemini

You will have some choices to make this month, and they may have major, far-reaching consequences. But you can consider things from all sides, and make the right decision. Stay calm, don't forget the details, and be patient when the wave carries you forward!

Work. You're facing a difficult task at work – take up the fight or leave the game altogether. No one would blame you, if you opted for the latter, but it is unlikely to happen. Closer to the end of the month, you will find your all your work was not in vain.

You might face some obstacles this month that throw a wrench in your plans. They might look differently, depending on your past, and each individual situation.

Those with longstanding ties to colleagues from other cities or countries will tackle various problems that are likely to seriously hamper your path forward.

Alternatively, legal issues loom on the horizon, or perhaps a secret will come to light, either for you or someone in your circle.

These are all things you will have to deal with for all of February, but near the end you will be able to untangle it all and get back on track.

Money. Financially, February looks to be relatively neutral. You are not expected to receive large amounts of money, but your expenses are predictable and within your means.

Love and family. As far as your personal life is concerned, you can expect to run into some problems. Many will have disagreements with family members, and though this is more likely to occur with your in-laws than your own relatives, that is not always the case.

You may discover many things – starting with some unpleasant moments involving your relatives. They might also find out something about you, which will have a negative influence on your relationship.

The stars recommend all Geminis keep a close eye on their words, actions, and avoid any risks to their reputation. That applies to all other areas of life of interest to you, as well.

Health. The main danger you're facing this month is the road. All month long, particularly from the 11th to the 20th of February, be very careful when driving and traveling, whether far away or close to home. Accidents are highly likely, as are other unpleasant incidents.

Cancer

When your chances of winning are so low, is it even worth trying? Is it better to take a break and wait for circumstances to improve? This time, it's worth taking a step back – don't bang your head against a wall – sometimes, it is made of reinforced concrete!

Work. All of February, you will see significant constraints on your ability to act, and people you counted on may not behave as you would have expected. It will become clear that you will have to pay too much for services you did not plan on needing.

You might encounter serious financial disagreements, unexpected demands, and complaints you will have to address. On top of all that, you will face a lot of unclear, incorrect, or intentionally misrepresented information. On top of that, during this most difficult month, it is not worth making any major decisions, so put your plans off for the future.

Hold off until March! Then, you will have a better grip on the situation, and things will be more favorable to you. Everything in due course!

Money. Against this backdrop at work, your financial situation cannot be sustainable. You might be bleeding money constantly, and in some cases, that will be due to business, and in others, your personal life will be at fault. In the most difficult cases, both will cause you problems.

Love and family. If your interests are entirely wrapped up in your personal life, you should steel yourself for what lies ahead. Many will face difficult financial situations, when trying to settle debts and pay off credit, and this will have a negative effect on the entire family.

Couples will also face real hurdles. Different outlooks on life and value systems, along with all of the financial problems will lead to resentment of each other.

The only ray of light during February's dark days is your positive relationship with colleagues, friends, and relatives living in other cities or abroad.

If life hits you over the head, take a step back. Soon, you might go on a trip – that will give you some headspace to clear your mind and calm down.

Health. Those who are spared by problems at work or at home might find themselves dealing with health issues instead. Old, chronic illnesses may get worse, or new maladies may unexpectedly appear. Avoid anything involving danger, and remain observant about everything.

Leo

Should you make a concession or fight to the end? The stars recommend the former. Sit down to negotiate, and bargain, one thing at a time.

Work. The trend you're dealing with this February is disagreements with business associates, which may have begun in January, if not earlier.

Just as before, this will stem from differing opinions on the development of your work, and who it belongs to. Your position is not so stable, so lean on friends for support, as well as anyone else up to the task.

Don't rush things – you are unlikely to resolve any of this now, and things look like they can be put off for later.

This of course pertains more to entrepreneurs and managers, while employees may encounter changes in their place of work. That may be due to changes in leadership, new directions, or new people as well.

Many will face stiff competition and unfairness from management. Keep a close eye on your duties, and don't forget the details. Listen more and talk less.

This is not a time where "truth is born in a dispute". When defending your position, stick to the facts, and avoid getting into arguments.

Money. Your finances are likely to be neutral. Competing interests and ideas about money are not yet coming to light.

Love and family. Any unpleasant situations in February most likely involve your job, and problems are likely to bypass your personal life.

The exception to this is couples with shared business, who have already dealt with problems. This month, contradictions may worsen, and in some cases, lead to divorce or a separation of affairs, including real estate.

Health. You may find yourself worrying excessively and stressing this month, which is the most negative thing you can do to your nervous system, which, doctors believe, is the source of all illnesses.

During this challenging time, try to get enough sleep and remember, your health is number one, the rest will follow.

Virgo

This month, you're like a hamster in a wheel, which is as efficient as one would expect. In order to make more sense and less trouble, you need to hit the brakes, look around, and come up with a detailed plan for what you're going to do next.

Work. This month, you may face a whole range of problems. It may be outright associates in other cities or abroad acting with outright hostilities, or legal problems looming on the horizon. What's more, managers will face strange behavior or open hostility from subordinates, and employees will deal with intrigue from colleagues.

During February's stormy seas, only those closest to you will be able to give you any support, so when you need it, it makes sense to ask them for help. If you are grappling with serious legal quandaries, don't let things snowball, turn to a good attorney for advice. The stars recommend doing it earlier, rather than later.

Money. This month's financial situation is likely to be uncertain.

Despite the ups and downs at work, you are not expected to face money trouble, and for now, things are expected to remain the same.

Love and family. Things are quieter at home, than at work. Those in a stable partnership will work together to overcome recent problems that continued into this month.

However, couples who fail to deal with the harmful influence of the stars in the second half of 2020 may have to address the painful issue of separation, and they likely won't manage without lawyers!

In any case, your children can keep you going – they have a positive influence on all families.

Health. In February, many Virgos might feel less than confident and cheerful. Those who are weak are at special risk. This month there is a likelihood of old, chronic illnesses getting worse, and new, unexpected ones from appearing.

Trips planned for February may turn out to be unsuccessful, and bring nothing but problems. The stars suggest not hitting the road unless absolutely necessary, and postponing any travel until late February, or even better, March.

All month long, drivers should be especially careful, especially from February 11 to 19. There is a very high chance of accidents and other unfortunate incidents.

Libra

Your loved ones are highly aware of what words, and, more importantly, actions, push your buttons. It's not worth succumbing to that kind of manipulation, as it can lead you astray.

Work. Entrepreneurs and managers at every level may have to resolve a number of issues related to land and real estate in February, and that will be very difficult to do. Most likely, it will involve prices or other obligations, which will be the opposite of what you were expecting and counting on.

However, after those difficult discussions, closer to March, things will clear up a bit, and as you discuss the terms of a future agreement, hold strong, even if it is not always easy.

This month, things are likely to be neutral for employees, though it is not particularly promising or successful. There will be setbacks everywhere, along with paperwork, the right people will be missing, and other issues holding you back at work.

Things will improve closer to the end of the month, and the sky will be clear in March, as long as you are attentive, avoid mistakes, and don't try to rush things. Doing so will get you nowhere, right now.

Money. Financially, things are coming to a head in February. You will be spending constantly, and in much larger amounts than you had anticipated. That may be due to work, or your romantic or family life. In any case, closer to the end of the month, you will have a rather empty wallet.

Love and family. Many Libras are mainly interested in their personal life, and that is where most of your problems will be concentrated. Those with families will attend to their children's problems, and that is where the lion's share of the family budget will go. However, in addition to expense, children can cause difficult family relationships, and in some cases, quarrels. In other cases, your children will face serious problems, and you will have to put all your resources and effort into fixing them.

On top of all that, couples who were already on the rocks, as well as divorcing married couples, will have serious disagreements related to housing. In that case, things revolve around your supposedly owing large amounts of money.

Couples may also find themselves in a critical situation. Right now, relationships are very difficult and you are literally just holding on. Many simply will not withstand the pressure from the stars, and will end up in all-out conflict, before ultimately parting ways.

Health. You shouldn't expect any health problems, though this month will be somewhat emotional, which will lead to you feeling rather lethargic and depressed toward the end of the month. If that is the case, try to get enough sleep, and spend more time in nature. That can help keep you healthy in body and spirit.

Scorpio

February will force you to take a long, hard look at everything happening around you Keep a stiff upper lip! As always, restraint, a cool head, and stamina will save the day.

Work. This month, entrepreneurs and managers at every level are dealing with delicate negotiations involving your business partners. In some cases, this may include discussions about terminating the relationship, dividing ownership, and, most of all, about land or some other kind of real estate.

You will not be able to reach an agreement this month, and most likely things will drag on after a series of conflicts, and reach a stalemate that is almost impossible to resolve.

In time, however, the planets will settle down, and decisions will become clearer and easier. While things are calmer, collect all the documents you need for work, don't rush anything, and frequently remind yourself – slow and steady wins the race.

What's more, hold the defense, keep a cool head when facing hostile enemy attacks.

Employees may see negative changes in the workplace, and as a result, feel like they are between a rock and a hard place. There is no point in looking for a new job, now, so just hold tight, until the clouds clear over your head, which is bound to happen. It just won't be this month, so you'll have to wait it out a little longer.

Money. Your financial situation is difficult, and you are likely to incur serious losses, but nothing is for sure, yet. It is, however, very possible in the future, so there's a case for doing all your calculations in advance.

Love and family. Complicated situations which began at home earlier are continuing. As always, bitter, divorcing couples will divide up their home, while others will be fighting off crooks of all stripes. Things will drag out and might become somewhat clearer next month. In all cases, the stars recommend turning to family. You really need their influence and support, right now. They will not deny you their assistance, whether moral or material.

Health. This month, you aren't particularly energetic, but fortunately, you won't get seriously ill, especially if you take care of yourself and remain vigilant.

Still, be attentive and take care – don't get into any conflicts in public, and avoid any dangerous situations.

Sagittarius

This month, you will have to grapple with a variety of circumstances in your surroundings, most of which will be unpleasant. All of this may, however, open up new doors to better understanding. After all, every cloud has a silver lining!

Work. Entrepreneurs and managers of every level may face two serious problems this month. One of them will be a difficult relationship with colleagues from other cities or abroad, and it is very likely the issue will be certain obligations that were not entirely fulfilled.

The second problem will be a subordinate behaving strangely. Those who, according to their job description and responsibilities should be there to assist you are suddenly doing something other than what you had expected.

As things are winding down, many will have to deal with debts, obligations, paperwork, and stagnation everywhere you turn.

You will be dealing with this all of February, and things will only become clearer at the very end of the month.

Employees will face problems with their colleagues, and this may include incorrect or deliberately misrepresented information, gossip, and intrigue.

Money. Closer to the end of the month, your financial situation will improve significantly, and you can expect to receive the largest sums of money on February 28 and 29. In addition to your own earnings, someone may repay you an old debt.

Love and family. If your interests are more focused on your personal life, this month, buckle up for trouble with your relatives. It may involve debt, mutual obligations, and other promises made to each other.

Another real possibility is that someone from your family will end up in a tricky situation, possibly involving an illness, and will need your help. Of course, you will be there for them.

Moves to another city or abroad will be difficult. This may be due to laws in another country, dealing with stacks of paperwork and documents, or, in the worst cases, legal problems.

Health. This month, beware of accidents, injuries, and be very careful, especially when traveling or driving. Trips, whether for business or pleasure, may not happen, or may instead bring disappointment. The period from February 14 to 22 is particularly unlucky for you.

Capricorn

It's best you come up with a well-thought-out and detailed plan of action this month, as it is bound to be difficult and full of conflict. This is the only thing that can save you from disaster, whether at work or at home.

Work. This month, be sure to double-check any information, and don't take anyone at their word. Otherwise, you run the risk of being dragged into various problems- most of all, financial issues, which, in February, will come to a head.

Entrepreneurs and managers will have to settle some real estate, as well as various services. These bills may be higher than you expected. From February 7 to 20, many Capricorns will likely face losses, so take any steps possible to shield yourself, and don't rush things. Take the time to carefully check each account before signing anything and making a final decision.

Money. As stated above, February is a disastrous month, and this may be due to work, or possibly your personal, romantic, or family life.

Love and family. Many Capricorns will see major developments in their personal relationships.

Families will experience continuing problems involving their children. In many cases, children will behave inappropriately, which will lead to conflicts and huge expenses. Keep a very close eye on this sensitive facet of your life, as the problems are unlikely to end this month, and will instead continue into the future.

Alternatively, you will have to help your youngest family members, and that help is likely to be material in nature.

A real storm bodes for couples this month, and if the relationship was already hanging by a thread, February is the month that thread may finally snap. However, after arguments and separation, you may reconcile, which has happened before.

Health. Most of the month, you are feeling somewhat sluggish, and February's unstable atmosphere may drive you to a serious nervous breakdown. Remember, doctors agree that your nervous system is the cause of all ailments. So, try to remain calm, keep a cool head, and remember the wise words of Solomon – "This too, shall pass".

Aquarius

Your birth month arrives, right when you are ready for battle. The time has come to speak up for your rights!

Work. Aquarians who work are torn between what they have worked so long to achieve, and whatever is holding you back. But without a solution for past problems, you are unable to move forward, and this is something you'll have to accept.

Entrepreneurs and managers, for example, will have to answer important questions related to construction, land, real estate, and doing so will be a difficult task. For various reasons, you will find yourself in situations where doing what you set out to do is almost impossible – at least this month.

This may be due to active resistance from others, or just circumstances, but that does not mean that you should give up. On the contrary! Keep going! Victory is on your side, though you have a lot of ground to cover, and piles of documents to review.

Employees will endure difficulties at work. They should be attentive when it comes to documents, and avoid conflicts with management. Do not get snide with your colleagues, if you plan on remaining at your job in the future. If you do not, however, ignore this advice. Moreover, if your boss is planning on dismissing you, it might happen right now – but you won't be without a job for long; a new one will find you soon.

Money. Money matters will improve near the end of the month, and expect to receive a large amount on February 22 or 23.

Love and family. Many Aquarians may see major events take place at home or in their families this month. It is highly likely that this inextricable situation involves real estate, and all of your family members will be dragged into it.

This may be related to family quarrels, divorce, or separation of property. Or, you may fall into the clutches of a crook, dishonest people, or something unexpected will happen to your home.

In any case, be very prudent, and avoid any possibility of *force majeure*. Be most careful from February 10 to 24.

Health. In February, you are feeling great, and that makes it possible for you to tackle everything during this challenging month.

Pisces

During the month of February, you will find that you are facing limits on your ability to act freely. You need to collect yourself, and take a long, hard look at the situation, before waiting it out. Don't be rash, and instead act gradually, like a courtier at the royal court.

Work. This month, a difficult situation that came up somewhat earlier, will reach its peak. Entrepreneurs and managers at every level are finding their secret enemies and competition suddenly in action, attempting to throw a wrench in the gears of anything you do.

You may face intrigue, and incorrect or deliberately misrepresented information, which will have a significant influence not only on your work, but on your reputation, as well.

Those with ties to colleagues in other cities or abroad will also face trouble. Perhaps your partners will not follow through with their responsibilities, and generally display hostility. Alternatively, *force majeure* will somehow change circumstances, making it difficult to cooperate.

Trips planned this month will be unsuccessful and bring nothing but trouble,

February is unlucky for employees, too. Expect misunderstandings with those around you, inappropriate behavior on the part of colleagues, rumors, intrigue, and gossip. During this time, old friends or someone influential may support you. This also applies to situations where old legal troubles rear their heads again, which is highly likely this month.

Things will get better closer to the end of the month, when you will be able to be more productive and active.

Money. Against this backdrop at work, financial stability is simply unrealistic. Your income is dropping, while your expenses grow, and this will continue into next month, too.

Love and family. Those who are more focused on their personal life this month will also face difficulties and challenges. Many Pisces will run into conflict with their family members. They are playing by their own rules, and you are playing by yours. It seems that you don't share the same goals, and reconciliation will not be possible this month.

Your relatives may find out something you would have preferred to keep a secret, and that information will make it difficult to smooth over the relationship. A major blowout is highly likely in mid-February, but the relationship isn't over – next month, you will be sure to find a way to reconcile.

In any case, keep your cards close, and things will be better if you remember that early on. This applies not only to spouses, but also to lovers, whose relationship is under pressure from the heavens.

Health. You are feeling incredibly lethargic this month, and those who are already weak need to be especially careful. Old, chronic ailments may return, or unexpected health issues may arise.

Young and health Pisces should also be careful, and take steps to avoid injury or accidents. Be attentive when traveling or driving. The most dangerous period for you is mid-February, from the 10th to the 14th.

March

Aries

The scenery is changing in March, the skies are clearing, and you are feeling calmer. There's a way out of any situation!

Work. March is an ideal time for resolving any difficult situations that recently began. Complaints from your friends or superiors are becoming less relevant- maybe you found a shortcut to reconciliation, or perhaps the problems in question have simply faded away. In any case, things are moving forward for you, and that's already something positive!

During the first twenty days of March, you will be able to calmly resolve any difficult financial issues and receive a handsome sum of money.

The last ten days of the month are a good time to renew contact with colleagues or old friends in other cities or abroad. You might take a trip or start preparing for one.

Employees might take a brief vacation, and restore their nerves and emotions after the obstacles you overcame last month.

Money. Your finances are looking up in March. Money will be coming in regularly, and not only from official sources. You can expect support from parents, your spouse, or a loved one. Alternatively, you can count on sponsorship and credit.

Love and family. When it comes to your personal life, you can count on one of two differing outcomes. Either you will be able to shelter from the storm under the broad, strong wing of a loved one, or you will find yourself licking your own, self-inflicted wounds.

In any case, March will be a bit calmer than earlier months were. Many Aries who quarreled with their friends and partners earlier will find a way to reconcile. The second half of the month is particularly promising for this. During this period, you might also take a trip, or meet old friends living in other cities or abroad.

Health. You might feel less than sure of yourself and cheerful this month. Fortunately, you will have an excellent chance to leave work behind and get some more time to yourself. Take advantage of it, as there will not be many opportunities like it this year.

Taurus

Don't miss your chance – March is full of opportunities. Everything you were not able to do earlier, for various reasons, is happening now!

Work. A predictable, prosperous streak is beginning for you at work. Issues from earlier months are being resolved, some way or another, and your friends or superiors are playing a major role. With their assistance, you will be able to strengthen your position, and make significant advancements. Thanks to friendly intermediaries, you will be able to reestablish relationships with colleagues in other cities or abroad, and reach important agreements.

Employees may strengthen their position at their current workplace, or, if they need to, they will find a safe landing elsewhere.

In any case, you will be appreciated, needed, and in demand. You will be responsible for deciding a lot, you are in your place, and doing what you can do. For those who can't imagine life without work, this is the most important thing!

Money. Improvements at work will inevitably be reflected in your finances. You are earning more, and someone may repay you a debt, or perhaps you will find money you had forgotten about. The last ten days of March are the most promising for this. Expect to receive the largest sums of money on March 20, 21, and 28-30.

Love and family. You are beginning a quiet streak at home. Aggressive Mars is leaving your sign, and you are becoming softer and more easygoing. You still don't have any time, but try to find a few days, hours, or minutes to be with your loved ones, and they will respond in kind.

Single people, and those who have been disappointed in love before may meet someone interesting, and, most likely, that will happen when you are among friends, traveling, or with people who have come from afar. To summarize, you will not be bored, and your only problem will be finding enough time.

Health. This month, you are healthy, energetic, and incredibly charming. Everyone who crosses your path will take note.

Gemini

This month will take you right to your edge – but that is not a bad thing. You are on the right track, and the stars are on your side. It seems your time has come!

Work. When it comes to work, March is one of your best months of the year. Your previous problems are nearly resolved, and the path ahead is wide open. Entrepreneurs and managers may conclude favorable transactions and significantly expand their area of activity.

Thanks to your own efforts, difficult relationships from afar will improve a bit. Closer to the end of the month, you are likely to go on a trip, and this time, it looks to be very successful.

Employees may significantly improve their position at work, and may even be promoted. In some cases, this will happen at your current workplace, and in others, somewhere new. Here, everything depends on your plans and intentions. The ball is in your court!

Money. Financial problems are not on the horizon this month. You are making more money, and can expect to receive the largest amounts on March 3, 4, 11, 12, 22, 23, or 30 and 31.

Love and family. March is very work-oriented for you, and you may not have the time or energy for love. But this is not a problem- your loved ones understand, and you will be even closer when things settle down for you at work. Near the end of the month, you will have a chance to go on a trip together, and, even if it is short, you are sure to enjoy yourselves.

Health. Mars is in your sign, which means that you have more than enough energy, and the stars strongly advise you to use it only for peaceful means.

Cancer

In a way, March feels like a bridge between your incredibly difficult past, and hope for the future. In any case, you can finally see a light at the end of the tunnel, though it will initially be rather dim.

Work. This month, the fight over property is slowly fading away. The time has come to lay down your swords, and sit down to calmly solve the problem. Managers and entrepreneurs who have been struggling with adversaries for some time may do this. In March, you might reach an acceptable compromise, and make actual progress, once you have shown some flexibility. Of course, that is not necessarily the end of things, but just a few steps can go a long way to resolving longstanding problems- and that is a good thing!

Your relationship with colleagues from other cities and abroad is developing rapidly, and you may go on a successful trip.

Many Cancers are concluding a difficult cycle at work and at home, and are now looking toward the future, new goals, and business.

Employees are thinking about a new job and taking their first steps in that direction. The luckiest of them will be successful by late March or April.

Money. Your finances have somewhat stabilized. Closer to the end of March, you can count on old debts being repaid, and income from real estate transactions.

You may receive credit or payments from a division of property- and this applies to both businesspeople and quarreling spouses with shared assets.

Love and family. Many developments are underway in your personal life. The way things stand, divorcing couples realize they have done everything in their power, but nothing new they try is likely to work out. Your spouse is also tired of the fight, and ready to give something up. Seize the moment, and look for intermediaries. They may be attorneys, or someone closely related to you. Also accept that the world is much more favorable to you on the other side, and you have almost no chance of winning any protracted battles.

Those in stable marriages may go on a trip together, where they are likely to have a good time.

Health. Your energy levels will improve somewhat in March, and even those who fell ill last month are now quickly feeling themselves again. Nevertheless, the stars recommend you keep taking care of yourself and remain observant- your body is likely to experience more pressure from the heavens in the near future.

Leo

You have been fighting hard for a long time, trying to find a safe path. The time has come- you will either leave things as they are, or give up what you have been fighting for. Of course, the latter is rather unlikely.

Work. March is a period of transitions for Leos with jobs. Striving and overwhelming stress are things of the past, and looking ahead, your future is somewhat blurry. You may be determining your own place at work, convincing your adversaries, and, with the help of influential friends, achieving at least a part of your goals, if not all of them.

Employees can count on management being understanding, and decent compensation in case of dismissal.

The most promising time for all relationships is the second half of March, particularly the last ten days. This is when you will see significant shifts that will determine your future.

Money. This month, many Leos can count on money from a business partner, receiving credit, or dividends from a profitable investment.

Outside of work, you can count on assistance from parents, loved ones, and monetary compensation in cases of divorce.

Love and family. March is a rather promising month for your personal life. Stable couples support each other in everything, and those who engaged in a war of words in February can now see that their differences are minor, and they in fact share similar outlooks.

Those who have opted for divorce may discuss major financial issues, as well as their children's future. This time, things will go smoothly, peacefully, and, possibly, favorably.

Health. For most of March, you are feeling a bit tired, perhaps even lethargic, fatigued, and in a difficult emotional state much of the time. The stars recommend taking care of yourself physically, avoiding catching a cold, infection, and living a healthy lifestyle. Additionally, your loved ones are facing real problems and may need your attention and care. If you are driven to the very limit, then at least get enough sleep, which will let you regain your strength, as you'll need a lot of it this month.

Virgo

In March, you are feeling sociable, energetic, and doing everything you can to clean up the problems that arose last month. And you'll manage to do a lot of it!

Work. Virgos who work will move mountains this month. The difficult issues you dealt with last month will be resolved, one way or another, most of all, your relationship with colleagues from other cities or abroad, as well as legal matters.

You may receive help from loyal, well-meaning associates, acting as intermediaries or assistants. Thanks to your joint efforts, you will manage to get a lot done, and make great strides.

Trips planned for this month will be rather successful, but the hostile attitude of your colleagues from out of town or abroad will have changed for the better.

Employees will do much to strengthen their position- management will notice how your colleagues are supported by your work.

Money. Your finances have improved somewhat. Money is coming in regularly, and you can expect to receive the largest sums on March 1, 2, 9, 10, 20, 21, 28, and 29. During the last week of the month, your expenses will increase, but they will likely be reasonable and necessary.

Love and family. March is a rather pleasant time for your personal life. Single people are very likely to meet someone new- perhaps while traveling or among people visiting from afar.

Storms in quarreling families have faded away, and that may mean that everything has been resolved and doesn't need to be discussed, or simply that everyone has reconciled. However- that peace is very delicate, unreliable, and may fall apart at any moment. You are treading on thin ice, so try not to mess this up!

Health. This month, you are feeling sluggish, and the weak and elderly should be especially vigilant.

There is a very high risk of old, chronic illnesses returning in March, so take care of yourself, and if you need to, only let yourself be treated by a doctor you trust. This year is not particularly auspicious for you, and spring- February, March, and April, is especially likely to present challenges.

Libra

You can do it! Seize the opportunity in front of you and try to squeeze everything you can out of it. The stars recommend it!

Work. March will be full of significant professional decisions and intense responsibility at work. If you want to reconsider recent working conditions and agreements that do not serve your needs, now is the time to do it. Your adversaries and enemies will reach a compromise, as long as they have no other options. You will have to make sacrifices, too, but they are minor, and you can negotiate something much more beneficial to yourself.

March is the month when managers at every level, as well as entrepreneurs, can count on their subordinates, and employees can lean on colleagues. This isn't a frequent occurrence, so take advantage of the moment!

Near the end of the month, you will deepen ties with colleagues in other cities or abroad, and reestablish communication that had stalled, or perhaps take a successful trip. Overall, your professional life is improving, and the outlook for March is very positive.

Money. Your finances are also improving, as your expenses fall and income grows. Expect to receive the largest sum of money on March 3, 4, 12, 13, 22, 23, 30, and 31.

Love and family. Your personal life is also getting better, and though your children are causing a lot of worries, the problem doesn't seem unsurmountable. It appears you have found a way out, and that is already a plus.

You may send your child to study somewhere far away, or perhaps you simply send them away for school or to join the army. Whatever it may be, you have found a solution, and that is the most important thing.

Near the end of the month, quarreling partners may find a common language and forgive each other for past mistakes.

Many will go on a trip, and it looks to be a good one.

Health. March is an excellent time for you to take good care of yourself, take stock of your physical health, and, perhaps, think about heading to a health resort in the near future. You can think of how to live a healthy lifestyle and start applying it, either completely, or at least in part.

Fashionistas can work on their wardrobe and possibly even update their image. The stars strongly recommend anything aimed at improvement.

Scorpio

You are feeling freer and more adventurous in March. Your creative approach and out-of-the-box thinking are letting you handle everything February threw at you. There's nothing you can't solve!

Work. Some events looming ahead this month will have major, lasting, and, most importantly, positive results. Entrepreneurs and managers at every level will be able to negotiate with their stubborn adversaries with regard to difficult tasks involving land or some other kind of real estate. Everything has a price, and this time, it will be enough to smooth over a conflict.

During all of March's events, you will see support from your family members, as well as some other loved ones.

As always, you've got it all under control!

Money. Your finances are improving, but not from your salary or other earnings. This month, you may receive credit, sponsorship, or some other benefit from a real estate transaction. Those who are not involved in the business world may see help come in from relatives or other loved ones.

Love and family. You can also expect things to improve on the home front. Warring spouses have found peace again; both sides are tired of arguing and other misunderstandings.

In many cases, children can play an important role as intermediaries, and their influence on the family ambiance is as notable as it is positive. If you have any disagreements on housing, they will optimize somewhat.

Those arguing with their parents may also let bygones be bygones and start reconciling. Generally speaking, fate is changing anger to mercy, and that is palpable in every facet of your life.

Health. This month, you are feeling energetic and have no reason to fear illness.

Sagittarius

March begins flat and somewhat melancholy for you, but suddenly, things take a turn in the second half of the month, when things pick up and positivity reigns. The stars recommend pausing, looking around, and only then rushing into battle.

Work. Maybe you feel thrown off by a restless February, but March will be a new chapter. Developments over the last several years have made you more tempered and wise, and you no longer dive in headfirst. Difficult relationships with colleagues from other cities or abroad have greatly improved, thanks to your efforts. Responsible negotiations will take place near the end of the month, and you can expect a positive outcome.

Many will be planning a trip, for either late March or April. Additionally, your efforts may have smoothed over difficult relationships with colleagues and subordinates. Many Sagittarians will see strong allies appear this month, and with their help, you will be able to plan the future, while also tackling problems from the past.

Money. Your financial situation is looking rather neutral this month. Your expenses are low, and your income is modest and predictable. What's more, if you need help, turn to a business associate.

Those who are not involved in the business world may find support from loved ones.

Love and family. Your relationships with loved ones will turn out to be surprisingly fruitful this month. Many Sagittarians will find unexpected support right at home or from family members, and this help will be instrumental in resolving problems that began in February.

Difficult relationships with your parents will improve and become somewhat easier to understand. It is possible that your spouse or someone close to you will act as an intermediary, when reaching out to feuding relatives.

Trips planned this month may involve you grappling with major issues on improving your life in another city or abroad.

Health. During the first ten days of the month, your energy level is not particularly high, so try to look after yourself, get enough sleep, and spend time in nature on the weekends.

The last ten days of the month are most promising, and you are likely to feel sure of yourself, cheerful, and this will keep you going as you tick off your to-do list.

Capricorn

March will bring you a series of surprises, and this time, they will be appreciated. The heavens are starting to shine down on you.

Work. You're on a lucky streak at work. You have renewed ties with colleagues from other cities or abroad, and can expect a successful trip. This is the perfect time to work on your relationship with colleagues and subordinates, as well as management.

If you want to change something at work or look for a new job, now is the best time to do it. As they say, knock down every door, and someone is bound to open!

What's more, March is an ideal time for studying, creative activities, for example, touring new cities and countries.

Money. Throughout March, the financial landscape looks sustainable. You are earning more money, and expect to receive the largest amounts on March 1, 2, 9, 10, 20, 21, 28, and 29.

Expenses are less than they were in previous months, but right now they are related to your personal life- someone close to you or your children.

Love and family. You still have problems in your personal life, but this time, they don't seem insurmountable. Your children are better behaved, and their problems are easier to deal with. Couples' relationships are also calmer and more even, and if you are still together following a recent argument, then this is a good sign for the future.

If you have already separated, you are willing to take a step toward reconciliation. There is still hope of continuing the relationship.

Health. In March, you are feeling energetic and have no reason to fear illness.

Aquarius

You will leverage your energy and focus to succeed at all your tasks ahead. Right now, everything, or close to it, is under control!

Work. You will need to make decisions in March, which will have major, positive results. It seems that you are taking all past mistakes and shortcomings into account, and able to make the right choices.

Entrepreneurs will be close to resolving issues related to property disputes- over land or other real estate. Perhaps money will be your friend when handling this task. Perhaps you will be owed some kind of compensation, or, alternatively, you will offer it to your adversaries. In any case, things will take a positive turn, and turn out peacefully.

Closer to the end of the month, you will begin communicating with colleagues from other cities or abroad, and may take a trip or start planning one.

People will appreciate your efforts and support them, in both words and deeds.

Money. Most of your month will be dedicated to money, and for good reason! When it comes to finances, March is more than generous. Money will be coming in regularly, and not only from official sources. Many will see real profits from real estate transactions, whether buying, selling, or renting.

Love and family. Your personal life is much quieter than it has been in months. Any family quarrels are now behind you, and you can resolve important issues related to joint property or your home, at least in part.

Your relationship with your children is significantly better, and you may see your children who live out of town or abroad.

March is an excellent month for couples, and the last ten days, you might expect to take a trip together, or talk about going somewhere next month.

Many will renew ties with old friends, acquaintances, and former flames, including those who live in other cities or abroad.

Health. This month, you might periodically feel less than confident and cheerful, but things will not deteriorate to a serious degree, as long as you keep living a healthy lifestyle and get enough sleep.

Pisces

March is very kind to you. This is a time for action, and overcoming former obstacles. Grab life by the horns, you're finally having some good luck!

Work. This month, you will cleverly avoid several problems, and those you can't avoid will require attention and careful effort on your part. However, the situation will improve significantly, and the difficult challenges you faced over the last several months are now safely resolved- if not entirely, at least in part.

When it comes to resolving the most painful issues, you can count on support from old friends or high-level mentors. Thanks to their help, you will be able to work your way out of difficult legal intrigue, and grapple with both discreet and obvious foes.

Your relationship with colleagues from other cities or abroad will be much calmer, and you might even take a successful trip or finalize negotiations. However, don't let your guard down despite the positive developments. Not everything is fully resolved, and there are still some delicate matters to deal with that you will have to deal with later.

Money. Your financial situation is rather neutral in March. You might see some improvements toward the end of the month, specifically March 24 and 25.

Love and family. You can expect some positive changes in your personal life. Chaos, confusion, and various types of intrigue will come to an end, either entirely or in part.

Thanks to your efforts, and the help of friends, your relationship with your parents will be significantly better, and, thanks to help from some friends, so is your relationship with other relatives. In any case, hostile parties will suddenly hold their tongues.

Overall, your future is looking good, and new opportunities are slowly opening their doors.

Health. This month, your well-being is looking much better, and you are quickly on the mend from any illnesses you experienced last month.

April

Aries

You're on a winning streak, but that doesn't mean you can sit back and put your feet up. Take initiative, keep looking ahead, and the stars will help you at every turn!

Work. Your main task and true success this month will be developing your relationship with colleagues from other cities or abroad. You are facing almost no barriers, and are supported, necessary, and in demand. There is a real possibility of taking a trip which will be very successful, and will be instrumental in driving your business forward.

You may meet new friends, like-minded and influential benefactors. What's more, you are likely to reestablish old relationships, too. Thanks to your many backers, you are able to carry out your longstanding plans, and (in some cases) even think about moving or acquiring real estate somewhere faraway.

Money. Your financial position is looking up, and that will become very apparent the second half of April. During this period, you might see some unexpected successes and real blessings. You might even try your luck and buy a lottery ticket – it will pay off in dividends for the very luckiest.

Love and family. Your personal and romantic relationships are also expected to improve significantly. There's no harm in dreaming this month – on the contrary, it's quite useful to you. Single people and those who have been disappointed by past relationships will be particularly lucky. You are highly likely to meet interesting people in every respect in April, and one of them may become your one and only. In many cases, that will happen on a trip, or while with people who have come from afar.

April is also a good month for couples and lovers. Many will have a chance to see a place they had dreamed about for a long time, and that will have a most favorable impact on the relationship.

April is also a good month for reconnecting with old friends and partners, so keep this in mind if you recently broke off ties with someone for various reasons.

Health. You are going at full throttle, but despite your busy schedule, you're not feeling tired. You are full of strength, energy, and attention from others will boost your mood and self-esteem.

Taurus

You're about to make some major decisions, and you will learn more about them closer to the end of the month. Your main ambitions will be satisfied!

Work. The first half of April seems like a general rehearsal before the premier, or taking a giant leap forward. You may make arrangements with a friend or someone socially prominent, regarding a promotion or significantly expanding your authority. According to the stars, this is likely to happen during the second half of April.

Entrepreneurs may expect a favorable transaction with partners from their inner circle, as well as colleagues from other cities or abroad. Expect a successful trip during the second half of the month, and to sign promising agreements.

Money. For most Taureans, your financial situation has improved significantly. Money is coming in regularly, and suddenly there is more of it.

In addition to earnings from your usual place of employment, you might also receive profits from various sources. Your expenses are down this month, and predictable, as well.

Love and family. Though work is taking up most of your time this month, your personal life is very pleasant. First of all, single people and those who have been disappointed by former partners will have someone new in their lives. You won't need to set aside time to look for them, either – everything will happen on its own, while you're with friends, colleagues, or somewhere else where you can let your hair down.

Everything is calm for families right now, your loved ones are happy for your successes, and ready to help in both words and deeds.

Health. You might be feeling less than confident and cheerful during the first half of the month, though you have no reason to fear illnesses, as long as you watch your lifestyle, and remember to get enough restful sleep.

During the second half of April, you will suddenly be much more energetic. You are also more charming and attractive, and everyone is taking notice.

Gemini

Events in April will unfold in such a way that you will have your many talents on full display.

Work. Your greatest achievement this month will be the bright, positive development of connections with colleagues from other cities or abroad. You bring a lot to the table here, and your efforts will be successful.

You may have both allies and assistants right now, but at some point, they might become your friends, or benevolent and high-ranking supporters. By working together, you can move mountains! Though that may not even be necessary – perhaps the mountains will move toward you!

For all work activities, the first half of April is the best period, so try to plan major events during this time.

During the second two weeks of the month, things are also going rather well, though you may face a few problems, which you will fortunately be able to overcome. It is possible that after all this good luck, you will have to examine the details and administrative matters, which is never easy.

Money. Despite your professional success, moneywise, you are stagnating. This is temporary, in all cases. A bit later on, everything you are doing now will translate into a breakthrough, so work on the future, and believe in your star!

Love and family. Something interesting is underway in your personal life. Any moves planned this month may resolve most of your problems, and you will deal with the rest later. You may take a trip or move during the first half of the month, and during the second half, you will get to tackling your everyday problems.

Single people and those who have been let down by love in the past will have a magnificent opportunity to organize their lives. You are highly likely to meet someone who will change your life in April, in some cases that will happen while you are traveling or with people who have come from faraway.

Couples will be able to strengthen their relationship, and get more serious about their future, consider marriage or living together, which is also a good thing.

Health. Most of April, you are feeling energetic, healthy, and charming, which will not go unnoticed. You might start to feel a slight drop in energy around the last ten days of April, so the stars recommend that you slow down a little and pay attention to your body and its needs – rest and sound sleep.

Cancer

The stars are replacing anger with kindness in April. After some recent stress, you have an excellent opportunity to stabilize your position and you can't let it pass you by!

Business. As far as business is concerned, April is one of the best months of 2021. Entrepreneurs will be able to reach a peaceful alliance with adversaries, and even receive compensation for some recent losses.

The best time for you is the first half of the month, when you will be able to resolve everything peacefully, without any arguments, complaints, or disagreements.

Also expect offers during this period that might bring dying businesses back to life.

Employees will have a good opportunity to strengthen their position where they are, or find a new place for their talents.

During the second half of the month, you may experience some problems with friends or superiors. The most likely reason – money or failure to fulfill one's obligations. But despite the fact that these issues will initially appear insignificant, remember that they may return in the near future.

Money. April is very lucky for you, financially. You are earning more, and in addition to your usual earnings, you can count on old debts being repaid, credit, and also funds from business partners.

Those who are not involved in the business world can expect support from their spouse or loved ones. Many will also receive profits from real estate deals.

Love and family. Your personal life is on a quiet streak. Divorcing couples will reach a mutual agreement on real estate and housing, and in all cases, you will be able to resolve some of these matters this month.

Stable couples will be able to answer day-to-day matters related to real estate.

During the second half of April, many Cancers will meet someone new in their social circles. Single people can count on an exciting but, alas, short romance.

Health. You are noticeably more energetic in April, and even if you were recently ill, you are well on your way to recovery.

Leo

Your big win this month is moving ahead and changes. Thanks to that, and shifts in the stars, you can move mountains!

Work. April will have you pushed to your limits, and thanks to your tenacity, you will be able to resolve a number of your previous problems and be successful in your current tasks.

You are seeing your connections with colleagues from other cities or abroad develop, and you might take a trip. You will also see constructive negotiations with partners from far away.

This update will reach every area of your activities, and previous disagreements with adversaries will start to look like they are a thing of the past. This also applies to legal problems.

Despite the favorable trends, during the second half of April, you may once again run into friction with your foes. This time, things won't be as heated and tense, as your position is now stronger, and other, more promising opportunities are on the horizon. All of this may overwhelm your opponents, and their hostility will subside.

Employees will face a real, promising opportunity for a better, more favorable job, or to strengthen their position where they are. Overall, your professional life is stable, and that is definitely a plus.

Money. Your finances are also favorable this month. You are making more, and expect to receive the largest amounts on April 3-5, 13, 14, 22-24.

Love and family. Along with your financial and professional successes, April might also be lucky when it comes to romance. Many Leos will reconnect with old friends, including those who live in other cities or abroad. You may go on a successful trip. Mutual friends might introduce you to someone interesting, and, it's very possible this meeting will be fateful.

All month long, you will sociable, charming, and your friends and colleagues will take note. Wherever you go, you will be received with open arms, and all you need to decide is where, how, and with whom you prefer to spend your time.

Even those who have recently quarreled with their spouse can think of a way to reconcile, and here, your friends, relatives, and children may be a big help. If you do not want to spend your time alone, and you don't want to keep falling into the same trap, this month is the time to discuss some respectable conditions for retreat.

Couples in a stable relationship might go on a trip together, and it will bring you closer together.

Health. This April, you are much more energetic than you were before, and are on the mend from any illnesses you may have experienced last month.

Virgo

This month, the stars recommend you rethink the recent past to reach some necessary conclusions. If you work, only do so as part of a team!

Work. Big changes you were recently hoping for might finally be underway, right now. The results will not be overnight – the hardest part is getting started. In all cases, this month, you will be able to count on your business partners- their help will be effective, and material, as well as moral. This might give you new perspectives, and also give you some relief.

Difficult relationships with colleagues from other cities or abroad are looking better somewhat, though there are still some periodic and minor disagreements during the second half of the month. They will be resolved favorably.

Those facing longstanding legal problems will envision a path toward an agreeable solution. Employees might improve their relationships with colleagues as well as management, and also have a good chance of finding a new place for their talents.

Overall, you can expect improvements in all areas of your work, and that is a trend that will continue in the future

Money. Your financial situation has stabilized. Along with your usual sources of income, you can also count on support from business partners, and on receiving rather favorable terms of credit.

Those who are not involved in the business world can count on assistance from loved ones.

Love and family. Things are quiet at home, right now. Stable partners are able to help each other out in every way, by leaning on wisdom and love. In cases of health issues, you can count on your partner- he or she does everything he or she can for you.

Divorcing partners can resolve some issues related to housing and real estate, and this time, things will proceed calmly.

Many will go on a trip, which is highly likely in late April, or in May. Difficult relationships with relatives will slowly improve, and this is a positive process, which will continue in the future.

Health. This month, you are much less energetic, and you should be particularly careful if you are elderly or have a weakened immune system due to chronic disease. Your likelihood of falling ill is rather high this month, so caring for your health should be a priority. What a year!

Libra

Springtime flowers are popping up everywhere for you this month. Your dark days are over, you've turned a new page, and it is full of brightness and color. It seems that you've won another battle!

Work. This month you have a real chance to take a new look at the terms of a recent agreement. You have some room to maneuver, so you might try to bargain for something more favorable if you had given up too much.

Your relationship with partners in other cities or abroad has improved significantly, and that helps out with business, as well as your own image. With some flexibility, you can turn enemies into allies, as they'll have to deal with you, anyway.

Any trips planned this month will turn out very successfully; results may be even better than you expected.

However, the stars still recommend that managers keep a close eye on subordinates, and employees be attentive with colleagues. For various reasons – incompetence, poor faith, or ignorance, someone you were counting on might leave you disappointed.

Money. Despite the obvious upturn at work, this month you may face some financial problems. You will have constant expenses, and that may be due to your children, or possibly your personal life and family. In any case, you can comfortably say that this month, your expenses will be much lower than they were in February or March.

Love and family. Your personal life is also looking much better these days. Your challenges involving your children are partially resolved. And though you still need money for that, it is worth it. At the end of the day, you and those you care about will benefit. You might make some decisions – send your growing children to study somewhere, to work, or to live in another city or abroad.

After a difficult period, rife with conflicts, complaints, and grudges, spouses might reconcile. And even if it's not for the long term, that's better than nothing.

Couples and spouses might travel together in April. The trip will be successful and really bring you together.

Single people will have an opportunity to be the center of attention and find themselves a worthy partner.

Health. This month, you are feeling great and no illnesses are on the horizon.

Scorpio

April is a mosaic that you worked on for a long time, and the pieces are finally coming together. A promising future is now calling you, and all you need to do is decide where it will take you in the coming years.

Work. This month, entrepreneurs and management are able to grapple with difficult tasks that appeared recently. They might involve disputes over real estate, land, or other large assets. Though the squabbles have not entirely dissipated, the root problem is nearly resolved.

There is a lot of work to be done, and you will handle it carefully and responsibly, as always.

You might plan to take a trip, or to open business in another city or abroad in the very near future. Many Scorpios work in a family business, where parents or elder relatives may play a major role.

Money. April is rather quiet as far as your financial situation is concerned. In addition to your own earnings, you can also count on profits from favorable real estate deals, and support from business partners. Those who do not work in the business world can count on support from parents or someone close to them.

Love and family. Many Scorpios will see major developments at home and in their families. Those planning to move to a new home, city, or country might undertake important administrative tasks this month- such as concluding or continuing repairs, acquiring furniture, other items, or decorating.

Divorcing couples will tackle a number of property-related matters, but this time, things are expected to go more smoothly. You haven't achieved peace yet, but there is less conflict, and that trend will continue in the future.

Health. In April, you are not particularly energetic, so take care of yourself at all times, and remain vigilant. What's more- be attentive with your loved ones, perhaps your parents or other, older relatives will need help.

Sagittarius

You're being swept up in a flurry of events, and life is once again blooming in full color. God made you for transformation and travel, and your grand voyage continues onward.

Work. April is lucky for you, no matter which way you turn. You will quickly move forward, and one way or another, your problems from the past are resolving themselves. Your contacts with colleagues from other cities or abroad have become very significant, and you might take a successful trip.

Recent disagreements that were holding back your work together are still present, but things are changing, and fortunately, it's for the better.

Expect significant help in every area from business partners. Without a doubt, their influence throughout April will be a positive thing.

Managers at all levels should still keep an eye on subordinates and all of your team's work processes.

Employees should be attentive at work; the stars recommend avoiding any possibility of misunderstandings, blunders, or other, similar problems.

All Sagittarians, regardless of the field they work in, should check all documents over carefully, especially those involving a move, or collaboration taking place out of town or abroad.

Moves and business launches out of town or abroad planned for this month might lead to a big step forward for your business.

Money. Your finances are somewhat improved this month, and you will be receiving more money in the past, at regular intervals. Expect to receive the largest amounts on April 3, 4, 13, 14, 23, and 24.

In addition to that, you can count on a blessing which might look very differently, depending on your individual situation.

Love and family. April is an excellent time in your personal life, too. Your relationship with your better half or current partner is moving closer to ideal, something that doesn't happen very often.

Your children are in a good mood, and some long-awaited changes are underway. They are obedient and attentive. You may see your children who live in other cities or abroad.

Travel planned will be an important step in this direction. You might go on a trip that brings you closer to your goals, if you are currently thinking about major changes in your life.

Your loved ones may play an important role in your life this month – this includes your spouse, relatives, and former lovers.

Single people and those who have been disappointed by love in the past will have an excellent chance to change their personal lives. You will be a frequent guest at parties, celebrations, and you might make a strong impression on a member of the opposite sex. Attention and love are guaranteed – remember that and try to get out more!

Health. In April, you are bounding with energy and have no reason to fear any illness. April is an ideal time for shopping, a new look, and a trip to the beauty salon. If you are looking for someone new, get some exercise, as you won't find a better time than the present!

Capricorn

You are an excellent manager, and this month, your organizational skills will be on full display, both at work and at home.

Work. April is a busy time for you at work, and your biggest task will be the issue of major changes that will affect every area of your work.

Entrepreneurs and managers might think of a way to expand your business, and in some cases, that will lead to restructuring existing facilities, and in others, acquiring new ones. In either case, things will run smoothly and without a hitch.

Managers are able to count on knowledgeable, detailed, and responsible assistants and subordinates. Employees might be fully immersed in family affairs, but work won't wait! That is why many Capricorns will have to constantly juggle both work and family responsibilities.

Money. Financially, April is a successful month for you. Money will be coming in regularly, and you now have significantly more of it. In addition to your usual sources of income, this month, you can count on additional profit from various real estate transactions. Expect to receive the largest sums of money on April 6, 7, 15-17, 25, and 26.

Love and family. Your personal life is settling down, though you can't say it's exactly quiet. Many families will be experiencing problems with their children, and this may involve some expenses. But this time, these problems don't look quite so serious. The worst may be over, and things should get much easier from now on.

Many families are dealing with home improvement and day-to-day issues right now. That may be repairs, acquiring various household items, or decorating.

You may acquire some real estate, and in many cases, that will involve your children.

April is also a good month for couples. The challenges over the last several months are resolved, and you might go on a trip, which will smooth over any remaining conflict.

Health. This month, you are not feeling particularly energetic, so find some time to relax and spend time in nature. You will have a change.

Aquarius

You are both active and successful in April. Your energy and optimism are not only exemplary, but a source of joy for everyone around you. Keep it up!

Work. Everything is finally starting to go your way at work. Entrepreneurs and managers no longer have to pour their energy into last-minute changes, and you are sure to meet your goals. Jupiter is with you, and it won't make you wait long for a taste of success.

Your ties with colleagues living in other cities or abroad will become more important, and you might take a successful trip.

Those with longstanding legal problems will be closer than ever to an amicable solution. The same goes for those facing unresolved issues involving real estate, land, or other large assets.

It is fair to say that not all of your issues related to property will be resolved this month. Some disputes may continue throughout April, and beyond. But the worst is now behind you, and you can manage the rest at different points in 2021.

Employees can count on strengthening their position where they are, or unexpectedly being invited back to a previous job, where they also excelled.

Money. Your finances are modest but sustainable. Money is coming in regularly, and in acceptable amounts. Your expenses this month are both justified and reasonable: children, travel, and entertainment are the most likely.

Love and family. Your personal life is on a quiet streak. Spouses whose marriages are either rocky or in the midst of ending are tying up loose ends related to property and housing right now, but this time, the negotiations are peaceful. Both sides may have understood that a bad peace is better than a good quarrel, and act accordingly.

Your children are happy and your relationship with them is now warmer and better. You may see your children who live in other cities or abroad, or even take a trip together with them.

The second half of the month, you will be busy with home improvement, and this will continue into May.

Couples are having a wonderful time! They might also go on a trip which will be both fun and interesting.

Health. This month, you are healthy, energetic, and incredibly charming. Everyone around you will notice.

Pisces

The changes will continue this month, and this time, they are in your favor. Look toward the future with careful optimism, and plan things out well.

Work. April may bring major changes at work, which especially concerns managers and entrepreneurs. You may see real estate transactions, profitable purchases, or profitable sales, as well. In any case, you are on the receiving end, and that is reason to celebrate.

Those with longstanding legal problems will be close to an amicable resolution. Underlying issues here have not entirely disappeared, but are improving, and any loose ends will be resolved soon.

You will still find huge support at work from old friends or some superiors, and it will be both timely and effective.

Employees will strengthen their position at work and may even receive additional income.

Your ties to colleagues from other cities or countries are slowly improving, and you might conduct peaceful negotiations, which will relieve the pressure on your relationships, and open the door to a brighter future.

Money. Your finances are noticeably improving – in addition to your usual sources of income, many Pisces might count on support from parents, loved ones, and also additional profit from various real estate transactions.

Love and family. Your personal life may turn out in many different ways, depending on each individual situation.

Spouses in a stable marriage are solving important problems related to a move, or improving your home, cottage, or other residence.

Divorcing couples will do the same, but in this case, you are dealing with dividing property, particularly your home. This time, however, things will be free of conflict, and neither side will be pushed to the point of a showdown.

Any difficult relationships with relatives will get much better. It seems that things aren't quite so bad, and you can tackle the biggest issues without an argument, tension, or fuss. Now, both sides are ready to accept their mistakes, which is the true path toward peace.

In the near future, some situations may repeat themselves, but not as severely as during the first few months of the year.

Health. This month, you are not feeling particularly energetic, but if you keep living a healthy lifestyle and taking care of yourself, you should avoid any major problems. The stars still strongly encourage you to be careful when driving, and take precautions while traveling.

May

Aries

Your path is one of constant forward motion, and now, fate has given you no choice. As they say, no pain no gain!

Work. You have always been full of ideas, ambition, and now, you have more than ever! Business is moving ahead, your projects are underway, and you aren't facing any money problems. But luck is rarely ever entirely complete, so right now, a relationship with a friend or superior may be fly in the ointment. Most likely, the issue is money or other, similar financial obligations, and you will have to give up a lot – both this month and a little down the road.

Alternatively, you might just be the victim of fraud, at the hands of people close to you or someone you trust! For that reason, "trust but verify" is more than relevant this month!

Your relationship with colleagues from other cities or countries will become very important; long-term cooperation is likely being planned. In any case, a series of summer eclipses are pointing toward this, and one of them is happening right this month. That cooperation may have only varying success, but with time, you will overcome everything.

Money. Finances are going well enough in May; you will have money coming in regularly, and it might be a lot more than usual, too. You will not be able to escape some expenses, most of which are related to the uncompromising stance of a friend or mentor. You may have to give in at some point, as part of fulfilling past obligations, and this part will be excessive.

Love and family. Your personal life is stressing you out and jerking you around. Many families were planning building projects, and in some cases, that will take place in another city or abroad. More decisive Aries will be taking their first steps toward making that happen this month, while those who are more measured will plan everything out first, before diving in.

Your relationship with family will become more significant, and you may visit relatives living in other cities or abroad. Many will also meet up with old friends living far away. You may even go on a successful trip.

Single people might expect to be on the receiving end of some attention and romance, which might take place while traveling or among people who have come from somewhere far away.

Health. This month, you are feeling energetic and have no reason to fear falling ill.

Taurus

You are in fighting mode as you celebrate your birthday month. And you're right about that – you have to work hard and overcome a lot on the path toward reaching your coveted goals.

Work. Your position at work is growing stronger. Entrepreneurs and managers might count on bringing old projects back to life, and seeing your previous work paying off in the form of decent profits. You have new friends and mentors on the horizon, though you need to be careful with them. The stars suggest not making any hasty or rash promises, and not committing yourself to anything which might not be easy to follow through with later on.

Employees can count on support from friends and improved relationships with management. Not everything is a fairytale here, however – you have to deal with some grudges, so be careful and keep your eyes open.

Business trips planned between May 11 and 20 will go well, though your work will largely be resolved.

Money. Your financial situation this month is going well; you will be receiving money regularly, and much more of it, too. You might expect a raise or a decent bonus.

Love and family. Many things on the home front will be pushed to the back burner – work comes first! But during the first half of the month, those who can't imagine life without love and socializing might go on a trip with someone, or to visit an old flame who lives in another city or abroad.

Single people and those who have been disappointed by love in the past can count on meeting someone new and unusual during the first half of the month. Your romance may not last long, but it will definitely brighten up your life. Here, it all depends on you – if you want to continue the relationship, your partner will certainly not be against it.

Health. You are feeling energetic in May, and have no reason to fear falling ill.

Gemini

A good general always prepares for battle, and that includes the battlefield. That is the task lying before you right now.

Work. The first half of May will not be easy for you, you will have to overcome obstacles which may look differently, depending on each individual case.

You may be dealing with endless questions from associates in other cities or abroad. Or possibly, you will have to tackle complicated administrative matters, which may not always go smoothly. During the second half of the month, however, things will resolve favorably, and work will be moving forward steadily. This month, Jupiter, the lucky planet, is moving into the work-related sector of your sky, which means that you are ahead of the game, and things are going to turn out well for you. Some things may take place a little later than this month, but the most important thing is that they happen!

Money. Your finances are stable, but that's as much as you can say. You will not see any windfall this month, but your expenses are reasonable and within your means. You may get some small income from unofficial sources. In many cases, it will take the form of support from loved ones.

Love and family. The first half of the month is more suitable for personal, family matters, and many Geminis are busy with just that. You might relax with some family members, but it's best to avoid any travel this month – things may not turn out as you hoped and dreamed.

During the second half of the month, however, you have an excellent opportunity to travel, whether for business or pleasure. This is a wonderful time to meet new people, and to deepen existing relationships, too.

The May eclipse promises a new romance with lasting consequences. For single people, this may be an escape from many problems. But if you are already in a relationship, buckle up – the flames of passion may burn a lot hotter than you originally intended.

Health. During the first half of May, you are feeling sluggish, so take care of yourself and remain vigilant. Exercise particular caution when traveling or driving. There is a very high probability of unfortunate incidents and accidents during this period. During the second half of the month, things look brighter – you will feel more energetic and things will feel easier.

Cancer

May might just be one of your luckiest months in 2021. You have people on your side, and with their help, you can manage, if not everything, a lot, for sure!

Work. Favorable changes that began last month are continuing in May. You have new friends and mentors. With their help, you are able to resolve any remaining issues and think of different, innovative, and promising ideas. But be wary of excessive promises, even if they are coming from someone you consider a friend – their assistance may end up being a bigger burden than it's worth. For example, some of your earnings this month will go to pay for such services.

But Jupiter is moving toward a favorable sector of your sky in May, which means that your problems will be a thing of the past, and you've begun a new chapter that is sure to bring you new horizons. Right now, the door is slightly open at different times, and it will be fully open by December 2021 or in 2022.

Money. This month, your financial situation is up and down. You are spending constantly, and it may be due to business or your personal and family life.

Love and family. Your personal life is continuing the same trend that started earlier. Divorcing couples will be able to deal with the rest of their problems, but there isn't much left, and they may actually finish it. This time, old friends will help you during the negotiation phase, but that really depends on your position, so be patient and keep a cool head.

Stable couples will be able to face the new future together; they may start making plans, involving a move. During the second half of May, you can expect a lot of hassle related to your living arrangements, real estate transactions, and that will continue into next month.

Health. Most of the month, you will feel like yourself. You can expect some minor fatigue closer to the end of May, and you might need to take some time to yourself and get some decent sleep.

Leo

You're starting one of the best months of 2021! Some of the decisions you'll have to make now will have major and lasting consequences. Remember to look at the big picture, and you will make the right choices!

Work. This month, you are someone to envy at work. Entrepreneurs and managers will be making decisions about drawing partners' investments in their business, and most of your negotiations on that front will take place in May.

Alternatively, if you have divided your business, your partners might pay you for their share, and you will think about striking out on your own.

Employees are strengthening their position somewhat, and both management and colleagues are supporting you. That may signify a shift in your relationships. This is a good thing, though you will still face competition from a few people.

During the second half of the month, old friends or kindly superiors may play a very important role in everything. Their support is vital, but may be somewhat cumbersome for your bank account.

Money. When it comes to material matters, May is rather looking up. You will receive regular income, and it is significantly more, these days. The first half of May is particularly promising in this arena, when entrepreneurs will be able to count on additional profits, and employees can expect a bonus or severance pay, if they are dismissed.

This month, many Leos will be able to rely on credit, money from business associates, or other sponsorship.

Those who do not work in the business world will also be graced by gifts of financial Fortune. Parents or someone close to you will provide assistance.

Most of your expenses will occur during the second half of the month, and what you need to spend on will depend on each individual person.

Love and family. Your personal life is rather lively, these days. Stable couples might think about starting a family, or maybe buying a new home, too. For now, everything is in the planning phase, but they will start to take shape in the near future.

Couples whose marriages are on the rocks will take a step closer to divorce, and, most likely, dividing up their household.

During the second half of May, you might see old friends and former lovers, it is very likely that you will rekindle a relationship.

Health. This month, you are feeling healthy, energetic, and optimistic, as all challenges are passing you by.

Virgo

A new streak is beginning for you this month. Things will get easier, though you shouldn't let your guard down. You have a lot of work ahead, and a lot of ground to cover before you see your first victory!

Work. This month, your circumstances are changing, and the astrologist suggests it's for the better. During the first half of the month, your communication with colleagues from other cities or abroad are noticeably stepping up, and you might go on a successful trip. There are also changes in your circle – you are being supported by influential people, and in time, that assistance will become very real and effective. Right now, however, those people may not have a full comprehension of your business goals and objectives, so during the second half of May, you can expect some misunderstandings. Your task is to smooth over any discrepancies and listen to others who may turn out to be extremely useful to you in the future.

During the second half of May, projects that had stagnated for some time will come back to life, and finally start moving forward.

Employees might find a new job, and possibly even get a small promotion or raise. You might face competition, though, so it's worth being extra careful and attentive at work.

Money. The best time for your finances is the second half of the month, expect to receive the largest sums of money on May 22-24, 30, and 31.

Love and family. Most Virgos might still be more involved in work than in their personal lives. But things are changing, and that particularly concerns single people and those who have been let down by love in the past. They are starting to look for a partner, and those efforts will pay off in the near future.

Those in happy marriages will see that their relationship is growing stronger and deeper. A loved one may see some success, which will make you very happy.

Health. All month, you are healthy, energetic, and have no reason to fear any ailments. For the first half of the month, however, be careful when traveling and driving, as there is a very high likelihood of accidents during this time.

Libra

May is a time of deliberate decision-making for you, and you will strengthen your position, both at work and at home. The stars suggest staying on track and keeping your eyes on the prize!

Work. During the first ten days of the month, your job and career are far from your priority. You are more focused on home and family matters. But then, during the rest of the month, you will be more of a go-getter, and very responsible, too.

Managers and entrepreneurs at every level are making decisions about changing up their teams, and initially you will be looking at new associates. During the second phase, you will invite them to be part of the team. During the same period, employees might be given additional responsibilities, and the stars strongly urge you to take advantage of that. Your career is on the upswing!

You might also see shifts within your company, this time though, they will be reasonable and predictable.

During the second half of the month, you will noticeably begin communicating more with colleagues from out of town or abroad, and travel is highly likely. Despite the positive trends everywhere, when it comes to your relationship with faraway associates, trouble will arise. Fortunately, this is predictable, and not the first time you have dealt with this. You can expect dishonesty, poor faith, and outright deception. You will be able to overcome this, in fact, you are always able to maneuver out of these situations.

Managers should still be careful with subordinates and keep an eye on them as much as you can. Employees shouldn't entirely trust colleagues, and keep watching the changes playing out within your team. That is advice the stars have given you in the past, but, unfortunately, it is still relevant.

Money. Financially, May is relatively quiet. You aren't facing any money problems, and you may see income from various sources. This includes your regular earnings, and you might also count on profit from various real estate transactions, whether from sales or renting. You can also potentially count on support from a loved one or parents, particularly for younger Libras and those who live at home for one reason or another.

Love and family. During the first ten days of May, your own home will be the best place for you. You are supporting your loved ones, and they are supporting you, too. Don't take on too much work, and enjoy being around those you love. Visiting your cottage, spending time in nature, or going somewhere won't hurt you, either.

Families will continue to deal with problems involving their children, and, as usual, it ends up creating a huge expense. Right now, however, things don't look quite so serious, but there are loose ends, and you will have to deal with the consequences.

Health. In May, you are not feeling quite so energetic, and that may lead to bouts of lethargy and fatigue. If you have free time, try to relax and don't test your body's limits when it comes to food or alcohol.

During the second half of the month, be careful when traveling or driving, as there is a high likelihood of accidents.

Scorpio

This month, things are very much on your side. Your main achievement will be bringing contradictory elements of your circles together.

Work. For many Scorpios, May is a time for sitting down and negotiating with very different sets of people.

Problems related to real estate are still an issue, and during the first half of the month, you may be involved in disagreements and arguments, though things will calm down during the second half of the month. It is very possible that the thorniest issues will be resolved favorably by then. You can't say that problems will entirely vanish from your horizon, but gradually, you are overcoming everything, so be patient and stay the course.

Your relationship with colleagues from other cities or abroad are developing nicely. During the first half of the month, you may very likely take a trip and hold constructive meetings and negotiations.

Money. Your financial situation is still not stable, but you won't find yourself penniless. You may have some income from various real estate transactions, support from business partners, or a loan or credit on favorable terms. Those who aren't part of the business world might receive assistance from parents or loved ones.

Love and family. Your personal life may look differently, depending on the past and each individual situation. Divorcing spouses are still resolving challenging issues with regard to joint property and real estate.

Spouses in stable marriages will work together on challenging matters involving home improvement, and in some cases, the action may take place in another city or country.

In many families, there are major changes underway involving children – they are on a positive streak, and there is plenty of reason to be happy about that. And young couples thinking about expanding their family in 2021-2022 are laying out their life plans.

Health. This month, you are not particularly energetic, so avoid getting worked up, and be sure to get enough sleep. Spend more time in nature; it clears your head and cheers up your soul.

Sagittarius

Traditionally, May is a busy time for you at work, and this year is no different. Everything will be as it always is – while others are relaxing, you are moving mountains!

Work. During the first half of the month, your main task is overcoming challenging situations stemming from your associates in other cities or abroad. You will manage – things will work out in your favor during the second half of the month. During this time, you will see important and decisive changes underway. Many Sagittarians will lay out plans to expand their business, and in some cases, that may take place out of town or abroad. During other periods of 2021, these plans will come to life.

During the second half of May, expect another kind of contact to come in handy – you may reconnect with colleagues and old friends, or meet new people, as well. All of this will have a positive effect on your work, both now and in the future.

Money. Your financial situation is up and down. On one hand, money will be coming in regularly, and you will see more and more of it. On the other hand, though, your expenses are about to spike. That may be due to growing your business, or possibly from a situation in your personal or family life.

Love and family. May is a time of changes in your personal life. Many Sagittarians are thinking about moving, or buying real estate in another city or abroad, and taking decisive steps in that direction. You may reconnect with relatives, including those who live in other cities or abroad.

You might take a trip, meet with old friends, or people you have not seen in a long time.

All month, but especially the second half, is a great time for single people. There is a great chance of an interesting, possibly even fateful encounter. This is very likely to happen while you are traveling or among people who have come from afar.

Those who are already coupled up might see their relationship grow stronger, and love will take many to far-reaching places.

Health. In May, you are feeling energetic, but the stars strongly advise you to be very careful during travel and behind the wheel. You are likely to deal with difficulties in this area during the first half of the month.

Capricorn

Your family and personal relationships might become more important to you as the spring colors bloom. But remember to give yourself some breathing room your work will still be here tomorrow!

Work. The first ten days of the month are not particularly promising for work and financial transactions. The best thing you can do is deepen your relationship with colleagues in other cities or abroad, or even travel to meet them.

The second half of the month, you are busier and things are looking more positive, you might start thinking about ideas that for one reason or another were set aside, and the details on how to make them come to life. During this period, managers will strongly be able to count on their subordinates, and employees on their colleagues.

You will also see some major changes underway when it comes to work. Many will have plans to launch their business in another city or abroad, and eventually, these ideas will become reality. You will have to make a lot of changes though, for that to happen- the way you see things, get ready for the coming changes might be your theme for the second half of May.

Money. Your money situation is up and down, all month. A lot of your income will arrive between May 11 and 31, and expect to receive the largest sums on May 4, 12, 13, 22-24, 30, and 31.

You will have expenses during the first half of the month, and they will not be minor. Most of them will once again be related to your children or loved ones.

Love and family. Your personal life is also shifting. Parents are still worried about their children's futures and continuing to invest large amounts of money in their education and well-being. You are in this for the long haul, so get ready to open your wallet at any moment.

Many families are starting to discuss a move, and in some cases, these plans involve another city or country. Everyone will implement their plans differently, but things are unlikely to remain as they are now.

Your relationship with relatives is suddenly much more dynamic, and one of your close relatives might come visit you or, alternatively, you might see them where they live. In the case of couples on the rocks, things will get more complicated, and you can expect yet more conflict during the second half of the month.

The first half of May is difficult for couples in love, when for various reasons, they may see less of each other than they would have liked.

Health. This month, you are feeling good and don't expect any illnesses. During the second half of the month, however, be careful while traveling or driving. The likelihood of accidents during this period is rather high.

Aquarius

Your own home might become the best and most comfortable place for you this month. Communication with loved ones is comforting and pleasant. Happiness is not far away!

Work. As far as your professional life is concerned, the first ten days of May is not particularly promising. The best you can do is get your affairs and plans in order.

Builders and anyone who works with real estate and land in one way or another are exceptions to the general rule. Their business will be growing, and their income is, too.

May 11 to 31 is a good time to establish contact with old acquaintances, friends, and also bring old projects back to life.

This is also a good time for those in the creative professions. They might gain recognition in their fields, a positive development expected to continue into June.

Money. Jupiter is a lucky planet, and this month, it is moving into the financial sector of your horoscope, which means that you can count on seeing your income grow. That may be related to selling or renting out real estate, or possibly from receiving credit, loans, or other income from banking transactions.

Those who are outside of the business world can count on help from a loved one. Expenses are on the horizon the second half of the month, and they are not minor. Many will be related to your children, and their education, studies, or well-being.

Love and family. Everything in your personal life is going smoothly. Divorcing couples are consistently and fundamentally continuing the long process of dividing up their property and home. Gradually, this is bringing you closer to resolving your issues for good, but that is unlikely to be the case this month.

Couples in stable marriages are working together to overcome difficult real estate matters.

Your children are demanding your attention, and their needs will include large amounts of money during the second half of May.

The stars strongly recommend that couples take good care of each other, and are generous with one another. You should understand and accept that sometimes, that is what you have to do.

Health. This month, you are not particularly energetic, and that is particularly noticeable during the first half of May. During this time, many Aquarians might find themselves gaining weight, so be sure to stay active and spend more time exercising or going for walks in nature.

Pisces

Jupiter is a lucky planet, and it is moving into your sign, which means that things are shifting, and clearly for the better. Your life is about to change, so don't be afraid to dream – anything is possible!

Work. Many Pisces will connect their interests with colleagues from other cities or abroad, and most likely prepare for a trip. There are some bumps in the road though, which will look differently for everyone, depending on recent circumstances.

This is due to the international stage and other factors you cannot change. Be careful with documents, and check all necessary papers – this will avoid many problems, both now and down the road.

You will overcome these obstacles, assuming you make the right moves.

The most persistent Pisces will be sure to do just that. Additionally, you will likely be able to count on support from friends or superiors.

Positive developments are a real possibility closer to the end of May, around that time a lot of matters will resolve in your favor.

Some Pisces will think about changing jobs, or even starting a whole new career.

Entrepreneurs might expand their areas of operations, and in various periods throughout 2021, that is sure to happen. During the second half of the month, many will look for a location to develop their business.

Money. Financially, May is likely to be neutral for you. Both your expenses and income are predictable and reasonable.

Love and family. Many Pisces might try out another lifestyle. You might make big changes in your home – repairs, buying real estate, moving to a new house, or buying a cottage.

Your relationship with family might be far from ideal, during the first half of May, and you can expect disagreements and arguments. Only through the assistance of loved ones will you be able to put these problems to rest. You may not be able to fully reconcile just yet, but you can certainly count on a fragile peace to start with.

Health. This month, you are feeling energetic and shouldn't expect to fall ill. Even so, during the first half of May, the stars strongly recommend that you take care when traveling and driving. Accidents are highly likely during this time.

June

Aries

Pay attention to your surroundings while traveling, and keep your foot off the gas. The later you arrive at your destination, the better. It might be surprising, but right now, that's just how it is!

Work. The eclipse on June 10 will force most Aries, once again, to take a very close look at your associates from other cities or abroad. Even so, you are already used to the bumps in the road ahead. The problem isn't you, but rather the strange and occasionally contradictory behavior of your colleagues. This inconsistency, and potentially even dishonesty, will cause real delays as well as significant losses.

In order to mitigate these issues, it would be a good idea to be prepared early on, as you are fully aware of what is going on.

During this time, you can expect problems involving real estate, or other facilities, especially if you are a manager or entrepreneur.

In addition to this, many Aries will be dealing with intrigue, and unreliable or deliberately misrepresented information in June, so avoid any major decision-making until you get all the details and a clear picture of the situation.

Trips planned for June might not turn out quite as you had planned.

Money. Financially, June is not expected to be a particularly pleasant month. In the middle of the month, you might experience heavy losses, due to adverse circumstances, both at work and at home.

Love and family. Your personal life is turbulent and full of ups and downs. Your relationship with relatives is extremely tense, you might see unnecessary drama, conversations that go nowhere, and difficult revelations about your relationships. On top of that, your relationship with your children – both yours and your spouse's – is likely to sour. During the middle of the month, you may end up spending large amounts on the younger generation's needs.

Couples will unexpectedly realize that various outlooks on life divide them, along with differing value systems, and, potentially, financial problems. In a word, June is not likely to bring you much peace, anywhere.

Health. You are feeling energetic this month and are not expected to fall ill. The stars still strongly urge you to be careful when traveling and driving, as there is a high likelihood of traffic accidents.

Taurus

Things seem to be looking up these days, and you certainly have spared no effort in making that happen. You still have to fight for every step forward, and nothing is easy. But there is no way back, and there is nowhere to go but forward!

Work. Your biggest task this month will be fixing financial problems. You might see serious turmoil in this area, as you suggest one solution, and your adversaries want to do something radically different. This will require compromise, though others' unclear position will make it difficult for you to resolve things appropriately.

This situation will drag out, but it's not worth rushing things. Right now, you need to be slow and measured in your actions, and look at all the details.

Old legal problems may also crop again, alongside your demands at work.

Relationships with colleagues in other cities or abroad are also likely to run into problems, probably due to recent events.

Employees can expect disagreements with management, and here, you are more than a little at fault. Sometimes, you can be stubborn, unruly, and rigid. Even if you are right, there is a diplomatic and skillful way to explain things to your adversaries. That is the only way they will listen to you and understand. Remember this to avoid confrontation.

Money. June is full of contradictions when it comes to money; you won't find yourself penniless, but you might encounter misunderstandings and problems. Be careful with your friends and some superiors – their complaints might be excessive. And don't lend money to anyone, even your closest friends – later on, you might find yourself without any money, or any friends.

Love and family. You are also grappling with a lot of problems in your personal life. There is conflict and turmoil in your family and at home. Couples on the rocks are at war, once again, and this time, divorce is on the table.

The conflict is expected to peak the last ten days of the month, when aggressive Mars is in conflict with stern Saturn and unpredictable Uranus.

During this time, stable couples will deal with serious issues involving their home, including complicated repairs.

You might also face some difficulties with your parents and older relatives, which might look differently, depending on your past relationships and each individual situation.

Health. This month, you are feeling energetic, but toward the end of June, be careful, as injuries and accidents are likely.

Gemini

You're on full alert as you celebrate your birthday. That's not a bad thing, as positive changes are on the horizon, but first, you'll have to fight for them!

Work. This month, your ruler, Mercury, is in retrograde, so many of the things you have to work on are suddenly going much more slowly than expected. This is happening to all Geminis, regardless of their field.

Employees are planning on transferring to a new job, and that might involve somewhere faraway, moving, or active cooperation with associates in other cities or abroad. The possibilities of this development are encouraging, but during the middle of June, you will suddenly come up against obstacles that will throw a wrench in your plans. They may be laws from another country, unexpected, negative information sullying your reputation, or perhaps even force majeure.

Entrepreneurs planning to launch in a new country or cooperate with associates from out of town may run into similar problems. But thanks to your heroic efforts, most things will smooth over, and you will be able to deal with the rest, later.

Money. Your finances are up and down. Money will be coming in regularly, but your expenses are expected to increase. At the end of the month, however, you will see a positive balance, perhaps because of a large sum that will be coming in in both mid- and late June.

Love and family. In your personal life, you might face a whole range of problems. Your relationship with relatives has grown complicated – during the middle and end of June, you can expect serious arguments, which will drag your entire family into the fray.

During this period, some information will come to light, which will have a negative impact on your relationships, and force you to reconsider many of them. Alternatively, a relative might face serious problems and you will have to help them, in either words or deeds.

June will also be a challenging month for couples. They might find that it is difficult to see each other as much as they would like, or perhaps they will have trouble reaching an understanding.

Those who are moving somewhere faraway will face challenges to overcome in both June and July.

Health. This month, you might experience anxiety, stress, and an emotional rollercoaster, which will be reflected in your mood and well-being. Try to get enough sleep, and remember that excessive anxiety is not healthy. And remember to be extra cautious when traveling and driving, especially in mid- to late June!

Cancer

This month, once again, you'll be wading through a jungle of various problems. But will you finally understand how to break out of this vicious circle?

Work. June will force you to take a step back and seriously adjust your plans. Circumstances are working against you, and the best thing you can do is not rush things, and remember that slow and steady wins the race.

Many Cancers will have to work meticulously when it comes to studying and solving their problems.

Those with longstanding legal problems will face an unexpected twist. Some circumstances may change, which will significantly weaken your position. Your foes will be working, both openly and discreetly, and some undesirable information will come to light, with the most unfavorable influence on your business.

Additionally, you are once again facing challenges from a friend or superior, and, as always, money or other obligations are involved. Moving forward, you can say that things will smooth over a bit in July, but for now, you will have to deal with the problems at hand gradually, relying on patience and wisdom.

Money. Against this backdrop at work, your financial situation simply can't be stable. You will be spending money, constantly, and expect the largest expenses in the middle and at the end of the month. Be particularly careful if you work directly in finance – bankers, accountants, and brokers.

All Cancers, regardless of their field, should consider that any financial risk this month will end in major irreplaceable losses.

Love and family. Your personal life is also less than ideal. You might deal with serious disagreements with friends, and in some cases, you will even part ways.

Couples might find themselves arguing frequently, and if you and your partner have any skeletons in the closet, get ready for them to come out this month.

Slowly but surely, your life is heading toward major changes and separations, both with partners, and friends. It is unlikely things will remain elusive, as you are beginning a new chapter in your life. That will involve parting ways with certain people and things.

Many will consider moving in the very near future.

Health. If you manage to be spared trouble at work and at home, you might instead face issues with your health. The elderly and those with old, chronic diseases need to be particularly careful. This month, you might see things get worse, and what's more, it might become rather serious. Young and healthy Cancers might also feel under the weather – they may feel lethargic, fatigued, and depressed. If that sounds like you, take care of yourself, and remember, "this too, shall pass!"

Leo

The next few weeks you will receive a sign, that certain projects requiring enormous efforts are coming to an end. But you will not give up without a fight, and this move is the right one!

Work. Mars is in your sign, which predicts a serious fight. Entrepreneurs are, once again, dealing with partners' hardline views when it comes to business. Once again, this is over differing views of how you envision the business developing, and in the most serious cases, you will go your separate ways.

Serious conflicts are likely with your adversaries during the middle and end of the month, but there will be no winners, yet. The feuding parties are refusing to budge. Your position is weak though, right now, so take advantage of anything you can, in order to protect yourself.

Employees are likely to experience yet another disagreement with management, as well as hostile colleagues. You might be dismissed, but you are not likely to have much to complain about there; you will still have the last word.

Your friends or mentors might be a glimmer of hope during all these painful processes. But not even they are all-powerful, nor are they always consistent or even without their own interests.

Money. Your financial situation is looking neutral. No major losses are expected for June, but your income is modest. The stars recommend that you try to save everywhere, as summer might be expensive, and future prospects are especially vague.

Love and family. Your family and personal life is rife with problems, in the case of many Leos.

Your spouse or partner might be going through hard times, and really need your support, right now. Their reaction, however, to your initiatives, might not be what you had planned or deserve.

Alternatively, serious arguments are a real possibility, due to both sides' hardline positions.

Friends' influence will somewhat improve things, but is unlikely to entirely resolve the problem.

If the roots of this confrontation are something that took place long ago, then either now, or next month, you will be able to put an end to relationships that ran their course long ago.

Health. You are feeling energetic in June, and are not expected to fall ill. You might start to feel slightly more tired during the last few days of the month, but if you live a healthy lifestyle and remember to get enough sleep, you should be able to avoid any trouble.

Virgo

You should carefully plan out any major changes, if you want to avoid inevitable failure. The stars strongly recommend taking previous missteps into consideration and patch up any weak points – and they are definitely there!

Work. In June, you will need to take on a leadership role, in order to get out of a crisis. There is no other way, as no one around you has the same skill, experience, and logic.

Your main problem this month might be serious difficulties with colleagues from other cities or abroad. You may have thought that the situation was almost resolved, but problems once again reared their heads, only this time they are worse and more unexpected than ever. This complicates everything, and will make you reconsider your relationship with someone you once counted on.

Alternatively, you might see old legal problems cropping up on the horizon, and they may take a new, unexpected turn. Or new circumstances may come to light, seriously weakening your position.

In all cases, it is better to trust yourself, as well as people who have a prominent position in society. You may have some people like that in your life. But most likely, the situation will drag out, and only start to improve in mid-July.

Employees will fall into a trap of complicated intrigue at work, when colleagues bring up all of their mistakes and shortcomings, both past and present. Things will only improve when management gets involved, so take advantage of that wisely!

Money. Your financial situation looks difficult in June, but things aren't hopeless. You have a lot of expenses, but you also have money coming in, so there is reason to believe that by the end of June, you will be staying afloat.

Love and family. Your personal life might end up on the back burner, given how many major fires you are putting out at work. But when it comes to family, partners, relationships with relatives and loved ones, remember to be careful and attentive. Certain secrets may come to light in June, both yours and those of your loved ones. That will seriously complicate your relationships, and in some cases, will actually alter your fate.

In any case, things will be easier and cheaper if you conduct your business peacefully, so take any chance you get and remember – "bad peace is better than a good quarrel".

Health. You are feeling pretty good in June, but the turmoil around you this month will have an effect on your nervous system, which doctors believe is the source of all ailments.

Those with cardiovascular and spinal issues need to be especially careful – during the middle and end of the month, things are likely to worsen. Be careful during these periods while you are traveling or driving, as there is high chance of accidents.

Libra

June will be rife with problems and conflicts. Exercise restraint and be cautious, the only way for you to hold onto your position and resist your dogged opponents is by acting deliberately and systematically.

Work. Your main task in June is to deal with your colleagues in other cities or abroad. Once again, you are dealing with ambiguous, evasive behavior from your adversaries, and, in some cases, outright deception. You have been here before, so you already know what to do, and how to counteract your foes.

Along with this, the stars once again recommend that managers keep an eye on their subordinates. Their mistakes, which are highly likely this month, might seriously weaken your position.

Employees should be careful when dealing with colleagues and not accept any missteps at work. You might be given new responsibilities and it will not be easy to shoulder them all.

Travel planned for June might not be successful, and results will either be unclear or downright negative.

Money. Your financial situation is difficult and full of contradictions. Money might be coming in regularly, but your expenses are sure to increase. The astrologist predicts that most of them will be related to your personal and family relationships. Expect to pay the largest sums during the middle of the month.

Love and family. This month, many Libras are dealing with difficult family matters. Once again, this is due to your children, who might have yet another surprise in store for you. And once again, expect to pay the largest sums toward dealing with this problem during mid-June.

Going forward, your children are bringing you not only joy, but also strife, so be sure to keep an eye on this part of your life. Things will smooth over a bit in a year, but in the meantime, be sure to keep an eye on younger children's health, and older children's affairs. Certainly, when it comes to money for school, studies, or their well-being, there is no reason to be a miser – if not you, then who? Certain expenses are worth it.

In many families, there will be problems with relatives, most likely involving your partner's relatives.

Things are not easy for unmarried couples, either. You might run into disagreements for wildly different reasons – differing outlooks on life, different value systems, and, unfortunately, money matters.

Health. In June, you are feeling good, and there is no threat of disease. But the tumultuous ambiance around you might mean that later in the month, many Libras will feel fatigued and burned out. The stars recommend that you stress less, and remember to get enough sleep.

Scorpio

Any major change should be planned out carefully, and this month, you should be sure to check the strength of your plans. Be prepared!

Work. In June, most Scorpios are grappling with mundane, administrative issues. Entrepreneurs are continuing to rebuild their business, and are investing significant amounts into it. Additionally, you are once again dealing with problems involving an associate, and, as in the past, they are related to real estate or other large assets.

Looking for a way out of these problems might take up a large amount of your time, and, as always, the problem is month and compensation, a fact you will have to discuss at length. For many Scorpios, these events may take place in another city or abroad.

Those with legal problems will once again find themselves battling, and dealing with an onslaught of attacks from your competitors.

Money. Your financial situation is rather complicated. You can expect significant expenses, and, in some cases, they are related to resolving work-related issues, while in others, they stem from your home and family. You might get a small sum of money from various transactions involving your assets, or those of someone close to you.

Love and family. Your personal life is also not particularly peaceful, right now. You can expect serious problems with your home, and successful couples will fight this battle together.

On the other hand, those who have decided to divorce and separate might find themselves constantly arguing over who owes whom what, and what belongs to whom.

Those who move far away will have difficulty overcoming legal and everyday problems, such as laws in another country, and problems filing various documents.

It is worth considering that everything you do will involve delays and problems. You can expect red tape, or a lack of the people you need to carry out everyday tasks. This will affect every area of your life, and you can expect the same both at work and at home.

In all cases, be careful, never rush things, and don't forget the details.

Health. This month, you are feeling a little sluggish, so take care of yourself, and be vigilant. Remember to be extra careful during travel and behind the wheel, as there is a high likelihood of accidents this month.

Sagittarius

Pay close attention – this month you are running a risk of making both missteps and the wrong decisions.

Work. The influence of the eclipse will drive you to pay the closest attention to relationships with your business partners. You might face some ambiguous situations in this area of your life, which will make you question the reliability of your work together, as well as its entire future.

Negotiations will drag out, you might not have the people you need, and all the while, you will be grappling with red tape. If you are trying to launch a business in another city or country, or conduct various transactions related to expanding your business, this is where you might face disagreements with your partners. In addition, in mid-June, you are likely to run into problems brewing within your team involving associates and subordinates.

Alternatively, the team you manage is not ready for the transition you have been planning, and you will have to change things. The future has new things in store for you, which will force you to shift the way you work, your style, and management. Keep that in mind, and pay attention to the signs Fate is sending your way this month.

Money. Your financial situation is less-than stable right now; you are constantly spending money, with the largest expenses at the end of the month. Right now, money is coming in from various transactions involving assets or support from loved ones.

Love and family. Many Sagittarians will find that most of the excitement this month takes place at home. Changes you were planning for a long time are now knocking at your door.

Moves and plans related to buying real estate, and conversations about it all are in the background, all month long. You and your loved ones might experience certain disagreements about these matters. You can be sure that in time, everything will calm down and you will find consensus.

But you may have more serious matters on your hands in June – unexpected complaints from relatives, and problems involving acquaintances in other cities or abroad, if you are planning on leaving the country.

Alternatively, your family members may face problems that seriously disrupt your plans.

Couples might find themselves in a difficult situation, where their relationship is put to the test. Your partner might begin behaving strangely, and you should be patient and wait for things to blow over – they will, eventually.

Health. This month, you are not particularly energetic, so take care of yourself and be vigilant. Also, be careful while traveling and driving –

the middle and end of the month are particularly unlucky times, when accidents are highly likely!

Capricorn

Take a closer look around, especially at those closest to you. Take steps to protect yourself!

Work. This month, you might get carried away with new ideas and projects. It would be good for you to make sure that they are feasible, as you may confuse your fantasy with reality.

Many Capricorns might have plans involving faraway places and foreign countries, and during various periods of 2021, you will be taking your first steps toward making them a reality.

For now, though, you are in the planning stage, and can expect a lot of bumps in the road ahead. You will encounter some of them this month, and some a little later on. But you're tough, and not used to losing. So once again, you will overcome the obstacles and play by your own rules.

In any case, the stars strongly encourage managers and entrepreneurs to keep a close eye on subordinates, as trouble is brewing within the ranks, over the coming changes. You may also be dealing with red tape, a lack of people you need, and a lot of needless fussing around.

Employees should do their jobs carefully and be cautious when communicating with their colleagues. You might also be a victim of untrustworthy information, or pulled into unflattering intrigue.

Money. Your financial situation is up and down. On one hand, money might be coming in as usual, predictably. But expenses will unexpectedly rise. Most of the time, this is related to your personal life and your children's and loved one's needs. Expect to spend the most in mid- and late June.

Love and family. Your personal life is not stable, right now. Many families are once again dealing with a problem involving their children. Again, most of your budget is going toward the younger generation's needs, and it may happen more than once.

Couples can expect stormy skies, as well. Some relationships have simply run their course and will end this month. Whether the separation is permanent or temporary depends on you. Maybe you want to have the last word, and it will be harsh – but you will come to regret this, so don't burn any bridges right now. There is always time for that later.

Many Capricorns are clearly dealing with the prospect of moving, and this will become a reality a little later, in 2022.

Health. This month, you are not particularly energetic, so take care of yourself and be vigilant. Also, be careful while traveling and driving.

Aquarius

Do not be afraid to ask questions and clarify things, be sure to read documents and instructions closely, and treat your loved ones with care. If you follow this advice, June will go much more smoothly for you.

Work. June is not very auspicious for you at work. Things are better during the first half of the month – you might take a short vacation and go somewhere warm. If that doesn't happen, you might get your affairs in order, and take care of tasks you have had on the back burner for a while.

During the second half of June many Aquarians will once again deal with matters involving their partners – per usual, this involves disagreements over real estate, and once again, things will descend into arguments.

Regardless of how things play out, don't lose your own voice. Prepare your arguments and check your facts. The stars suggest that this time, you are right, and you will win out in the end. But this is a difficult time, and nothing will be resolved without arguments and a fight.

Money. Your financial situation might be uneven in June. You will be getting money regularly, but your expenses may be high. In most cases, this is due to your family or love life.

Love and family. Expect turmoil in your personal life, too. Divorcing couples might once again drag each other into battle over shared assets and, most likely, their homes. After a period of relative calm, your partner's aggression might throw you off guard, but the fact is, the war has not ended, and in fact, it is heating up.

In many families, problems are starting to appear involving children, and this will involve some expenses.

Stable marriages mean that couples are able to overcome various challenges involving their home together.

Couples are dealing with challenges, too. Be ready to compromise, and willing to accept someone else's point of view, if you value your current relationship. Right now, you might make some errors in judgment, so don't react too harshly to a loved one's strange or erratic behavior. It's not really possible to get a clear understanding of the situation, so just try to hold tight.

Health. This month, you are feeling energetic and are not expected to fall ill. The stars still strongly suggest that women refrain from experimenting with any changes in their appearance, as it will bring nothing but trouble.

Pisces

June is a month full of contradictions. You may run into serious problems while carrying out your ideas. The stars recommend that you don't give up, don't rush things, and remember that slow and steady wins the race.

Work. When it comes to work, June is not particularly promising, especially the first twenty days of the month. This is not a favorable time for signing any contracts, or for making professional contacts with someone new.

Things are also looking gloomy when it comes to making requests to the powers that be. This is a good time, however, for meticulous administrative tasks, in order to bring everything into order.

The last ten days of June, things are looking up, but you still can't count on making any real progress at work.

During late June, many Pisces will face unexpected problems which might look very differently for everyone. There is a likelihood of unexpected run-ins with regulatory bodies, or old legal issues rearing their heads once again. Alternatively, you might deal with serious disagreements with colleagues from other cities or countries, and challenges while traveling.

You are unlikely to resolve these problems in June, and most likely, they will carry into July.

Money. Your financial outlook this month is not particularly favorable, as you can expect major expenses, and less income than usual. Most of your expenses will involve your family and home.

Love and family. For most Pisces, June will revolve around your personal life. You might expect stress related to home improvement, repairs, buying furniture, appliances, or home decoration.

The stars strongly suggest that you take your time with the most expensive purchases, and just get a good idea of everything you need until June 25. Mercury is in retrograde, so you might have to take back some of the things you bought.

In many families, once again, you are dealing with problems involving your relatives. The root of these issues began some time ago. Nothing new is expected, but old feuds will once again be resurrected.

Health. You are feeling sluggish in June, and during the middle and end of the month, you might face an unexpected force majeure. During this time, drivers and travelers need to be particularly cautious, as there is a very high likelihood of accidents.

July

Aries

July has you strongly focused on your home life. Things will work out beautifully for you, as long as you are careful and measured in your actions.

Work. This month is more about relaxation and plans with your family, and not particularly promising for work or your career. The exception is those working in construction or whose business is somehow related to real estate, hotels, and recreation.

Entrepreneurs will make a decision about expanding their business, and examine various possibilities for purchasing or renting real estate.

Employees will be more focused on their family this month, and the stars recommend that those who are destined to remain at work refrain from making any requests from the powers that be – now is not the time.

Your relationship with colleagues from other cities or abroad is moving along and changing for the better; some things will turn out, and others will not quite be as you hoped – just like anything else.

Money. Your financial situation might not look so stable in July. You will be bleeding money, and most of the time, this is related to your children or family.

Love and family. Your personal life is noticeably livelier, and definitely not calm. In many families, problems involving children are continuing, and there are likely to be expenses related to this.

The stars strongly recommend being attentive with your children, and leaving nothing to chance. This will do much to prevent any suffering on your part.

Most Aries are busy dealing with important issues related to home improvement. You are likely to buy a home or start building one, or at the very least, purchase furniture or items for home décor.

Couples will find their relationship has become very emotional, and not always harmonious, these days. The stars suggest you refrain from making too many demands! Complaining to your loved ones might have negative consequences, and might ruin the best days of summer for you. If something is really bothering you, remember the very useful phrase, "Yes, dear," and hold your tongue. Things will work out better, this way.

Health. This month, you are not particularly energetic, and frequently feeling tired or fatigued might lead to changes in your mood. If that is the case, be sure to get enough sleep, and spend more time in nature – summer is the best time of year to be outside!

Taurus

The last few months, you have been under the sign of constant self-improvement. Now, you have one more step to overcome on this winding road, but this time, things should go much more easily.

Work. As before, your main challenge in July might be your relationship with the powers that be. Things are complicated here – during the first ten days of the month, you are very likely to face conflict and other unpleasant encounters. You will share some of the blame for this – insisting on doing everything your way is not likely to make you many friends. Remember this and act accordingly.

From July 11 to 31, things will quiet down to a degree. You might go on a trip, which will turn out very successfully. And even if you are very busy with work, that is a good opportunity for a change of scenery and to distract yourself from your recent troubles.

Money. This month, money matters are mostly stable, and you will have money coming in regularly, as well as reasonable and predictable expenses. Expect to receive the largest sums on July 6-8, 16, 17, 24, and 25.

Love and family. Many Taureans will have to juggle work and family this month, as you will also face issues at home. In many families conflict is likely between parents and children and the reasons may vary. Rebellious children are always an issue, and there comes a time when all children try to break free of their parents.

Alternatively, your children might react to serious trouble between their parents, especially if things are moving toward divorce or dividing up your home.

Stable partners might still resolve difficult matters involving your home or other delicate issues involving real estate.

In all cases, the first ten days of July are the worst time as far as conflict is concerned. After July 11, things will calm down; many will travel then, and things will turn out well.

The best time for couples is July 11-31. During this time, you might take initiative and make progress toward reconciliation. This advice goes for those who quarreled with loved ones recently, as well.

Health. All month, you are rather energetic, which is making it possible for you to juggle everything this month throws at you.

Gemini

This month, the stars' positive and negative influences will seemingly engage in a fanciful pas-de-deux, and you will need to be flexible as you maneuver between them, in order to leverage the former, and avoid the latter.

Work. During the first ten days of July, you can expect to feel tense. Problems that were making your life difficult in the past will continue during this time.

Many Geminis will once again have to deal with inconsistencies from colleagues from other cities or abroad, which, in many cases, will once again drive many negotiations close to the point of breaking down. Can things turn around? Yes, and you will be the one to do it. Your efforts will drive necessary changes, and contribute to getting relationships back on the right track.

There are also positive trends afoot. From July 11 to 31, you may receive tempting business offers, whether you are an employee or entrepreneur.

For now, things are still in the negotiation phase, but they will certainly lead to success in the near future.

Money. Your finances are clearly improving, and you can expect to receive the largest sums on July 9, 10, 18, 19, 26, and 27.

Love and family. During the first ten days of July, prepare to deal with problems in your family life, too. During this period, a difficult situation from the past will continue involving your relatives.

This time, however, the issues may take an unexpected and very unpleasant turn. You will need to be flexible as you maneuver between two feuding family members, or resolve relatives' difficult problems.

This month, and especially during the first ten days of July, expect certain secrets to suddenly be brought to light – they may be yours or those of someone you know. This will complicate relationships, including for couples or spouses, if they have anything to hide from each other. Remember this, and keep a close eye on developments.

Things will calm down during the rest of the month. This is a good time for traveling, resolving problems that have appeared, and working on your troubled relationships.

Single people will have an excellent opportunity to meet someone interesting, and, most likely, that will take place while you are traveling, or among people who have come from afar.

Health. This month, you are feeling energized and are not at risk of falling ill. During the first ten days of July, however, be very careful while traveling or driving. There is a high likelihood of accidents and injuries during this time!

Cancer

The fight goes on! Patience is a virtue – and this time, you can reach your goals, or at the very least, work your way out of a complicated situation you find yourself in!

Work. During the first ten days of the month, you will once again be dealing with old problems. Expect to see your relationship sour with friends or influential people who have lent you a hand in the past. As always, things will revolve around money or other things of material value. You will not be able to reach a compromise, and something has to give. Do what you can, or you have a lot more to lose, both now and in the future.

Many Cancers are thinking of starting a new business, and in some cases, that will take place in another city or abroad. For now, it is just an idea, but in the next 18 months, it may become a reality.

During the rest of July, you can expect to go on a trip, or actively communicate with your colleagues from afar, regarding upcoming changes.

Money. During the first ten days of July, things will get ugly, and in many cases, that is related to your job. From July 11 to 31, things will look a bit better, though you will still need to be very careful, as problems from the past are still hanging over your head.

Love and family. Your personal life is tumultuous and full of turmoil this month. The first ten days will not be favorable to couples – the heavens will once again pressure your relationship, putting it to the test. You are well-acquainted with the reasons why, though an old problem may take an unexpected turn, so look at all your options, and take steps in advance. This is especially pertinent if you and your partner have shared finances.

Spouses in stable marriages are able to overcome challenges together, and this time, things will involve finances and your children.

During the second half of July, things will quiet down, and it should be smooth sailing. This will give you an opportunity to take a step back and look at things from a distance, enabling you to take steps to resolve them.

Single people and those who have been let down by love in the past can expect a passionate but short-lived romance sometime between July 11 and 31.

Couples who have split up might see a better future on the horizon, and, hopefully, they won't have to wait long.

Health. This month, you are feeling a little sluggish, and that is especially the case for the elderly, or those suffering from longstanding chronic conditions.

Leo

The best spot under the sun is never free. You need to examine this truth now.

Work. This month, the stars are urging you to pay attention to your relationship with business partners. Once again, conflict is brewing in this area of your life, and, most likely, it will come to light during the first ten days of July.

In some cases, this will involve the division of joint business, or some sort of compensation.

The stars recommend you haggle to the very end, and only then accepting conditions as they stand. But you are not likely to do that, so you may find yourself in a quagmire.

Alternatively, you may be seeking money to keep your business going. The astrologer does not envision this being particularly promising, but if you feel certain, then take this opportunity.

Employees might run into conflict with management, and think about another place for their talents. If that sounds like you, keep in mind that it may take a few months to find the right place, so remember to measure twice and cut once.

Money. Financially speaking, this month is rather challenging, though you will certainly not find yourself penniless. You will not see money coming in constantly, and are more likely to receive credit, sponsorship, or help from loved ones.

You may also get your share, if you are dividing up a business.

Love and family. During the first ten days of the month, your personal life looks tense and full of conflict. Of course, this involves couples who were already experiencing problems. Once again, you are thinking about divorce, but if you do not plan on ending the relationship, think about what you say, and avoid doing anything rash. If things have already been resolved, then this advice is superfluous.

Stable couples will overcome problems together, and that may include receiving help from a loved one, who supports you during difficult periods at work.

From July 11 to 31, many Leos might go on a vacation, deal with household matters, repairs, or interior renovations.

Stable families will also think about expanding their family, which will happen in the near future.

Health. This month, you are not particularly energetic, and that is most noticeable during the period of the New Moon, from July 9-11. Take care of yourself and remember that your health is the most important thing, and everything else will follow.

Virgo

There are times when you need to fight with all you've got, even if victory seems unlikely. It's never worth giving up!

Work. The first ten days of the month, you can expect a series of challenges at work.

Entrepreneurs and managers may, once again, have to deal with old legal problems coming back, and this time, there will be an unexpected twist.

Alternatively, serious disagreements with colleagues from other cities or abroad are highly likely, and, as a result, you can expect things to stall.

Yet another possibility is the law standing in the way of your plans.

In any case, during this difficult period, your friends or a superior might extend a helping hand. With that support, you will be able to overcome your challenges, and maybe even resolve them entirely.

You can count on this after July 11, when pressure from the heavens will let up a bit.

Employees may find themselves victims of complicated intrigue during the first ten days of the month, so they should be careful when dealing with colleagues, and listen more than they talk.

Money. This month, money is a difficult topic for you. You will be spending constantly, and can expect to earn very little. This situation may continue, so remember to be thrifty and try to cut down on expenses.

Love and family. Virgos can expect to face challenges at home, as well this month. You may have trouble with both your relatives, or those of your partner. What happens in each specific family is hard to predict, but you have dealt with these problems before, and likely know their root cause already.

The stars recommend that you take steps early, before things get too difficult.

If you have anything to hide, it is worth remembering that during the first ten days of July, "all secrets come to light". That goes for whether couples are married or not.

Health. It is worth keeping an eye on your health during the first ten days of July, when accidents and injuries are highly likely to occur. During this time, the stars recommend being careful while driving and traveling. It is worth considering avoiding any distant travel – it will bring nothing but trouble.

Libra

Some of the decisions you make this month will have far-reaching and major consequences. You will be able to take a step back and look at the whole picture, before making the right decision.

Work. You will grapple with major tension all month, and reach the maximum of your intellectual abilities, solving various problems, all month. You can expect a lot of work, and for most of it, you will be able to rely on your inherent brilliance and skill.

Entrepreneurs will consider starting a new business, and to do that, you will need to consider new colleagues. This is a long-term project that won't come to fruition overnight, but you are already taking your first steps in that direction.

Your relationship with colleagues from other cities or abroad is developing with varying success – you manage to reach some of your goals, while others will have to wait for a better time.

Employees may be given additional responsibilities, or think about looking for a new job. For now, that is still in the planning and discussion phase, but expect things to come through in the near future.

The stars strongly encourage you to pay close attention to those around you, your friends, and influential people in your life who might have helped you in the past. For various reasons, you may face moral or financial problems with them, now.

Money. Your financial situation is improving, but it is not entirely stable, yet. You might be spending constantly, and in some cases, that may be related to business, while in others, it is due to your personal and family life.

Love and family. You will continue to face problems from the past in your personal life. Once again, parents will grapple with issues involving their children, and this will lead to more unexpected expenses.

It's up to you, but in some cases, it might be worth tightening your grip on things. The situation is repeating itself, so try a new approach.

Couples are also having a hard time this month. During the first ten days of July, you might argue unexpectedly, over moral and material matters.

Alternatively, you will spend a lot of money on spending time together. Actually, why not arrange something special for yourself and your partner – vacation, leisure, travel, or shopping? If you take this option, everything will work out great!

In mid-July, Mars and Venus are together, which means you might expect a new romance, if your last relationship didn't suit you, or you haven't had one before. Even if things don't last long, you can at least expect a hot summer fling.

Health. You are feeling good in July, and there's no chance of falling ill.

Scorpio

You are diving head first, right into the cycle of events. This month, you are bursting with energy, strength, and are capable of moving mountains. Good luck!

Work. July is opening doors to new horizons for you, regardless of your field. New opportunities, new spaces, and escaping old problems – right now anything is possible!

All relationships will become more favorable to you during the second half of the month, when things will be developing quickly, without any problems or holdups.

But nothing is ever perfect – so during the first half of July, you can expect to face old problems, and once again, you will seek a way to resolve them.

Entrepreneurs are still dividing up property with their partners during the first half of July. It may be real estate, or maybe even property itself. Expect a real possibility of serious conflict at the beginning of the month. Once again, you may have to recognize that you are not going to reach an agreement, and you will have to work out a compromise.

Employees can also expect serious disagreements with management, or possibly even dismissal. But at the end of the month, you will be offered a new job, and it will be much more interesting than what you were up to before.

This new job may be related to organizations with an office in another city or abroad. You are likely to travel, and rather than causing you stress, it will be an opportunity to combine business and pleasure. Once your work is done, you will be able to see places you'd only dreamt about for some time.

Money. Your financial situation is ambiguous this month. Most likely, things will remain as they were, and you can expect the largest amounts to come in on July 20, 21, 28, and 29.

Love and family. Not everything is easy in your personal life. Expect the greatest challenges during the first half of the month, when you will see a conflict from the past continue into July.

This is most relevant for spouses, who were already having problems in the past. Once again, your problems revolve around disputes over property, probably real estate. If you want to resolve things peacefully, you can always turn to your children. They will have a positive influence.

Stable couples will be able to work together to overcome any problem related to real estate, in some cases, they will have to turn to a knowledgeable lawyer, though.

During the second half of July, things will quiet down significantly. There is a possibility of going on a trip, and getting away from the routine, gossip, and other troubles that followed you around in the recent past.

Health. This month, you are feeling fairly energetic, and this is most noticeable after July 10.

Sagittarius

It will be difficult for you to focus on just one thing in July – your attention is needed at home, for routine tasks at work and for longstanding problems. Concentrate and you'll manage. This time, you just have to get through it.

Work. During the first ten days of July, you will, once again, face issues that began earlier. That may be due to difficult relationships with your colleagues in other cities or countries, or possibly due to legal issues.

In some cases, these problems may be interrelated, which will only make things worse. This can put a damper on your ability to do your work to your full potential, especially if you have plans for a business launch in another city or abroad.

In addition to that, managers should pay close attention to their subordinates, and employees should keep an eye on their colleagues.

For various reasons, you may face problems involving these people, which will be reflected in your work, relationships, and much more, all month.

Things aren't so bad, though; during the last ten days of July, the challenges you faced in earlier will look somewhat differently – you will have a better grasp of things, and they will seem easier to solve.

Money. Finances are up and down this month. You won't see a windfall, and you will also have some expenses to deal with, so close to the end of the month, your wallet will be feeling pretty light. Things will look up in a month or six weeks, but for now, just be thrifty and modest.

Love and family. Your personal life is not exactly calm, either. Those moving far away will face a series of problems, including challenges involving documentation, or instability on the world stage.

You may have to consider various offers related to real estate, and in some cases, that will take place in other cities or abroad. Even if you can't decide this month, you will find a solution in the near future.

Your relationship with relatives is growing complicated, and you can expect serious conflict during the first ten days of July.

The best time for couples is the first half of the month. This is when you may take a successful trip, which will strengthen your relationship, and answer many questions about it.

Health. This month, you aren't particularly energetic, so try to get enough sleep and spend more time in nature.

A weekend out of town or a week at the beach would help you gather strength, while also give you a better understanding of your loved ones. The best time for that is the second half of July. During the first ten days, it is better to stay at home, as this is not a promising time for travel, whether faraway or close to home.

Drivers should be careful during this period, as well, especially on July 1, 2, 3, and 4.

Capricorn

July looks like a rehearsal before your big premiere. Everything that starts right now will take you down a positive path in the future.

Work. You are undergoing major changes at work. Many Capricorns are thinking about opening their own business in another city or abroad and taking steps in that direction. For now, you're in the planning stage, once you start moving toward your goal, things will come to fruition. You might take a trip, but you won't know how things will turn out until you're already there.

In all cases, you can expect your business partners, who have shown themselves to be responsible and reliable, to lend a helping hand.

Entrepreneurs and managers should keep a close eye on all documentation and paperwork, and also monitor their subordinates, as any errors on their part may throw a wrench in all of your plans.

Money. Financially speaking, this month might be a disaster. You will be bleeding money, and in some cases, your expenses may be related to business development, while in others, you can blame your personal life, likely either your family or children.

Love and family. Your personal life will continue to see the same problems you had in the past. Many families will be resolving matters related to their children, and the price tag will not be cheap. Take a look at every option, you likely know the root of your problems, and that is the most important thing if you are going to resolve things.

Throughout this, you can count on help from your spouse or someone close to you. Seeking common ground with your children will lighten their load.

If you are expecting changes with your children, someone close to you will provide assistance.

Many families are considering a move, and slowly starting to make plans in that direction.

Couples' relationships are feeling the pressure from the stars, and only those who truly live for love will go the distance.

For all relationships, the first ten days of July will be the most difficult period, when you can expect conflict to break out. During the rest of the month, things will quiet down significantly, though that is not exactly sustainable. Most likely, you will have to grapple with some problems and mitigate them, somehow.

Health. In July, your energy levels are not their highest, and those suffering from chronic heart or spinal conditions should be especially careful, as well as those with weakened immune systems for any reason.

Aquarius

July will bring serious challenges in fundamental areas of your life. Don't give in, even an inch, and try to hold onto what you believe is yours – this advice comes straight from the stars.

Work. Work is on a relatively tumultuous streak, right now. You may be seeing new opportunities, new business, and additional responsibilities. But you might also be grappling with problems that began last month and which might now take an unexpected turn. The focus is still on disputes over property, land, or real estate.

The most difficult period for this will be the first ten days of July, when you can expect conflict. Keep your cool, do what you can at work, and seek a compromise. Prepare your arguments, and base yourself on the facts. Each step forward will bring you closer to victory, so keep that in mind, and stand your ground.

This month you can also expect to see new opportunities, no matter your field. The future is just around the corner, and those opportunities will grow, as your problems diminish. Within six months, that will be very clear to you.

Money. Your financial situation will improve somewhat in July, and that is directly related to the additional responsibilities or new contracts you have been working on. You can expect to receive the largest sums of money on July 9, 10, 18, 19, 26, and 27.

Love and family. Your personal life continues to cause you trouble. Couples in the midst of separating or who have been on the rocks for some time will be dividing up their property, and can expect some serious arguments over real estate. Emotions will be running at their highest during the first ten days of July, when things will be most difficult.

During the same period, stable couples might have to fight off those who have been claiming property belongs to them. There is no chance of compromise now, and no one will win this. But fate will be on your side soon enough.

July will be kind to those who are looking for love. You can expect a passionate romance, especially between July 11 and 31. This is an excellent opportunity for single people to build their own destiny. Those who are already married or in a stable relationship might find themselves in a tricky situation – they will not succeed at trying to have their cake and eat it, too.

Health. You are not particularly energetic in July, so take care of yourself and be vigilant.

Pisces

Don't abandon your plans, even if you hit a wall, which you are likely to do. Keep your eye on the prize and stay the course. Be confident, but careful!

Work. During the first ten days of the month, things will be less-than ideal for you. Problems from the past will rear their heads again. In some cases, you may once again find yourself mired in legal problems, or possibly, you will face unexpected disagreements with colleagues from afar.

In other cases, this is not a problem that appeared out of thin air. You were aware of the situation, but things have taken a new and unexpected turn. Try to resolve painful issues without panicking, and keep a cool head. very soon, your troubles will be resolved, some way or another.

In addition, entrepreneurs and managers should pay close attention to their subordinates, as there may be intrigue among your team, which will carry over into the work itself.

In the case of employees, at any sign of intrigue among your colleagues, be sure to remain above the fray. You may put your foot in your mouth and see things get carried away.

Money. Your financial situation is up and down. You might be spending constantly, and in some cases, that is due to work, while in others, your personal life is the culprit. But you will not find yourself emptyhanded, and you can expect to receive the largest amounts on July 1, 2, 11, 12, 20, 21, and 28-30.

Love and family. If love or family is at the top of your priorities in life, you will have to deal with a whole host of problems this month Once again, you will face a challenging situation involving relatives, who may be ill or fall on hard times.

Alternatively, old arguments might crop up again, and this time, you can expect new information, which will simply add fuel to the fire. Someone close to you, your spouse, or children will smooth things over. One of them might reach out to hostile relatives, and facilitate the peace process.

July is favorable to couples, who might find themselves working together to overcome obstacles, and even deciding to live together.

Health. This month, you will feel much better than you have. The stars still strongly recommend being very careful while driving. The most dangerous time is the first ten days of the month, when you should also avoid any long-distance trips, as they will bring nothing but strife.

August

Aries

It's the dog days of summer, and you're juggling both work and family, and finding new opportunities with both!

Work. You have a tendency to get so invested in projects, that you make circumstances work in your favor. That's what's happening right now – you see a goal, and the planets line up in just the right direction. The heavens are coming to your aid, which means that you are sure to succeed. In all cases, managers and entrepreneurs are able to depend on their subordinates, and employees can count on their colleagues. This is a rare occurrence when everyone works smoothly and efficiently, as part of a team.

Employees will be on the receiving end of attention from management, which may lead to concrete, material reward.

Your relationship with certain friends, or influential members of society, is still less than ideal. The problem still revolves around finances or other obligations.

Things may not look very acute this month, but the underlying problems are still alive and well, and you will be reminded of that in the near future. Closer to the end of the month, however, a loved one or business partner may act as an intermediary. This support might mitigate the situation, but it is unlikely to resolve it entirely- but that's better than nothing.

Money. Your finances are looking better, and you honestly deserve it, after all your hard work. You can expect to receive the largest sums on August 1, 9, 10, 17, 19, and 27-29. You will also have some expenses to take care of, but the majority of them are related to something pleasant – vacations, children, loved ones.

Love and family. You can expect to deal with some problems rooted in the past, when it comes to your personal life in August. Once again, this is related to children, but this time, the situation is a little less acute, and much easier to handle. Conflicts will start to fade, and right now, that is the best you can hope for.

August is not a particularly joyful month for couples, but they will not suffer, either.

Those who are separated are unlikely to find a path to reconciliation, and things are likely to remain ambiguous.

Health. This month, you are full of energy and ready to move mountains. You will likely be able to find a few days and take a vacation somewhere, where you can enjoy bright sunshine and a warm beach.

August is a good time for shopping, creating a new image, or playing sports.

Taurus

The stars suggest focusing on yourself and your personal life in August. This month, your motto is – "my home is my castle".

Work. August is not particularly promising for you, professionally. The exception is those who somehow work with land, real estate, or recreation.

If that isn't you, the best you can expect this month is to get your affairs in order, and finish up all the tasks you had saved "for later". You will not be able to charge at full speed ahead until the last ten days of the month, which is the luckiest time for you. Employees will deserve recognition from management, while entrepreneurs will resume a project that was left unfinished.

The challenges of the last few months are slowly fading away, but they are not entirely gone, yet. During the last ten days of August, however, much will be resolved, and you should fully take advantage of this opportunity.

Your relationship with colleagues from other cities or countries is developing nicely, and in mid- or late August, you are likely to go on a successful trip.

Money. Financially speaking, August is not particularly auspicious, and most likely going to bring nothing but stagnation. Nonetheless, you can expect the largest sums of money on August 3, 4, 11, 12, 20, 22, 30, and 31.

Love and family. The best place for you this month may be your own home, and the best company may be your loved ones.

Stable couples will find success with their children, and any trips together planned in August will be turn out very well. You might see your children who live in other cities or abroad.

Divorcing couples will make important strides related to their home, and this time, things will be relatively peaceful and go off without a hitch.

Couples can also expect a good month ahead. You might take a trip together out of town, or to a tropical island, where you will get to know each other better.

Health. This month, you are not particularly energetic, and if you have any time off, be sure to take full advantage of it.

Gemini

The changes are continuing. In order to grow a new garden, you need to clean out the flower beds and weed. And that is exactly what you are going to need to do right now.

Work. During the first ten days of August, many Geminis can expect to face a series of problems. In some cases, it may revolve around overcoming legal issues, or possibly, involve colleagues from afar. In other cases, you will have to deal with another country's laws, over the course of the entire month.

During the second half of August, your main task might be conducting various transactions involving real estate or other property, which is particularly relevant to those planning a move or a business launch in another city or abroad.

Employees might carry out negotiations with counterparts from another city or abroad, but they will also have to overcome several obstacles, which will stall everything for a while. Things will even out by December 2021, but in the meantime, keep following your plans, and stay the course – don't even take one step away from it – you'll achieve everything you want!

Money. Financially speaking, this month is likely to be neutral. You have some expenses, but your income is also modest, and most of it is not from your normal workplace.

You can expect money from various real estate transactions, or assistance from parents or loved one.

Love and family. Your personal life will be full of unpleasant surprises during the first half of August. Once again, this will involve your relatives, and, in some cases, longstanding feuds, and in others, problems with close family members.

Those in the middle of long-distance moves will have to resolve various matters near the end of the month, and they will be related to your home. This will continue into September, too.

In all cases, you will be able to count on loved ones for support, both at home and at work. They may be your parents, spouse, or older relative. That help will be most noticeable during the second half of August, when many Geminis will have to outfit a new home. It is very possible that this will take place in another city or country.

Health. Your energy is running high in August, and you are not at risk of falling ill. Nonetheless, the stars strongly urge you to be careful when traveling and driving. The first ten days of the month will be the most dangerous.

Cancer

August will be like an intermediate step on your journey from a troubled past to a much brighter future. You will not see a real turning point until 2022, but remember, "every journey begins with a single step".

Work. Uranus and Saturn are still exerting strong influence, and that is most reflected in your relationship with your adversaries. This time, it's about large amounts of money at the root of a heated argument. The result of this might end up being positive – you might not get everything you want, but your enemies won't win.

The first ten days of August might be the most difficult period of the month. After that, the situation will improve to a degree, possibly thanks to mediators intervening – either attorneys or someone close to you. Their work will timely and valuable, and gradually, your problems will be resolved, one way or another.

Your ties to colleagues from other cities or abroad are developing nicely, and this will be most obvious the last ten days of August, when you might go on a trip or start planning one, or possibly hold interesting meetings and business negotiations. New people may be on your horizon, and their assistance will both resolve old problems, and simultaneously launch new projects.

Money. Your finances are up and down this month. Nonetheless, you won't find yourself penniless, and you can expect to receive the largest sums on August 7, 8, 15-17, 25, and 26. At the same time, you will have to settle debts, divide up property with your adversaries, and spend money on your children's and family's needs. Hopefully, by the end of the month, things will be back in order.

Love and family. The best time for your personal life is the last ten days of August. During this time, many Cancers might go on a trip with loved ones.

Your relationship with relatives will improve significantly during this period, and near the end of the month, you might see family members who live in other cities or abroad.

The first ten days of August will be challenging for couples. During this time, you can expect arguments going back to old problems. Each couple has their own, and everything will depend on your own situation. Most likely, longstanding problems are the cause, both for divorcing couples, or those who are still at war.

Health. During the second half of August, you are feeling energetic, and you are not at risk of falling ill. Even so, the stressful, tense situation during the first half of the month might cause tiredness and fatigue. The best cure for this is a good night's sleep and taking some time in nature.

Leo

You celebrate your birth month ready for a fight. And you'll get a lot of what you hoped for!

Work. The astrologist suggests that Leos might be able to get the most out of a tricky situation causing you trouble during the first ten days of the month. Once again, the problem is serious disagreements with partners over your joint business. If you face heated debates during this period, during the second half of the month, the thorny issues may be at least partially resolved. In some cases, the root problem will be financial compensation for dividing up your business, and in others, both parties will find an acceptable compromise.

Employees can count on a decent payout should they be dismissed, but many of them will negotiate something with management from their old jobs. In any case, you will be pleased with the end results, so feel free to pursue your desires.

Money. Finances are not looking bad this month, and you might even say that August is one of the best times of the year for you. You can expect to receive the largest sums on August 1, 9, 19, 20, and 27-29.

Love and family. Many Leos will see major events underway at work, and leave their personal life on the back burner. However, those who fate has connected to their spouse through shared work, might experience conflict over your business's future, or dividing it up.

You are only likely to reach a compromise during the last ten days of the month, when many relationships will be at their most effective and productive. When it comes to any difficult, controversial issue, you can count on support from your relatives, who might serve as intermediaries between divorcing or fighting couples.

Health. This month, you are significantly more energetic, and you are quickly getting better after any illnesses last month.

Virgo

Be careful in early August, this period is notable for its intense astrological activities. Just remember that during the second half of the month, Fortune is definitely on your side!

Work. During the first ten days of August, many Virgos will face a whole series of challenges. You will have to resolve legal issues, while also grappling with problems involving colleagues in other cities or abroad.

If you are not dealing with these matters, the stars warn that you should follow rules and the law to the letter, in order to avoid bringing problems on yourself.

Managers should pay close attention to their subordinates, and keep a close eye on anything brewing within your team. Employees should be careful in their work, and stay away from any workplace intrigue. You could easily get dragged into an unpleasant situation that gets much worse.

The stars believe that the best tactic from August 1 to 10 might be staying away from work as much as you can. Take some vacation time and spend some time alone and with your loved ones. If that doesn't seem realistic, then steel yourself for the open conflict to come. During the second half of the month, things will be more positive. You will have things under control, and play life by your own rules. This is also a great time to go on a trip, whether near or far, and for negotiations with the people you need. Complicated legal issues are also close to a favorable solution, as are any other problem that has been keeping you up at night.

Money. Your financial situation will improve close to the end of August, when Venus moves to the financial sector of your sky. You can expect to receive the largest sums of money on August 3, 4, 20-22, and 30-31.

Love and family. If family or love is the most important thing in your life, then be careful and keep your eyes open – during the first ten days of the month, you might come across undesirable information, with will have a negative influence on your relationship with loved ones. You may learn something unpleasant about them, or the information may be about you, instead. Examine the most delicate areas of your relationship and take steps in advance. If something happens, be sure not to jump to hasty conclusions. Just wait, and soon enough, things will blow over, and everything will fall into place.

Health. Anyone spared by professional or personal strife might suffer from health problems, instead. Take it easy and be careful to avoid injury from August 1 to 11.

The elderly and weak might see old, chronic conditions come back, and those who suffer from cardiovascular or spinal disease should be especially cautious. Drivers and travelers should be especially cautious, as well.

Libra

Friendships may play an important role this month. But you can expect more than just intimate conversations – partners and finances are fully under your responsibility.

Work. Traditionally, August is a time for a well-deserved vacation. But those who can't imagine life without work might manage to do a lot for their own business this month. Entrepreneurs and managers will take care of problems related to real estate and land, and be able to bring some things to order.

Your relationship with friends and some superiors will require both money and attention. You might consider certain expenses as a way to show your status, and others, in the eyes of the astrologist, will simply be superfluous. Take a look at your expenses, and reduce them, if you can.

Management and entrepreneurs should still be careful with their subordinates – one of them is either behaving unscrupulously or is simply incompetent. This is an issue that constantly gives you headaches and anxiety, so pay close attention to who is supposed to help you, but instead is slowing down your plans, ideas, and projects.

Money. Financially, things are up and down for you in August. You will be bleeding money, and most of it will be related to your home, children, or family. But it is highly likely that you will also see profits from various real estate transactions, either sales or rent.

Love and family. Family matters may be taking up most of your energy for the majority of August. You are still dealing with your children, and it is causing you a lot of stress. Once again, their needs may dominate your family budget.

Many Libras will be occupied fixing up their house, doing repairs, or acquiring furniture and other items for their home décor. In more serious cases, you will have plans for buying real estate, and in many cases, that will take place somewhere far away from your hometown.

Couples will have a tough time during the first ten days of August. During this time, you might have unexpected arguments, or certain developments might cool things off for you. Don't forget that you can change that, though! Be forgiving, patient, and generous, in order to avoid anything unpleasant.

August is a great time for vacations – take advantage, and go wherever you prefer – either a country home, or a tropical island will do! Summer nights are just as wonderful, either here or there.

Health. You are feeling energetic in August, and are not likely to fall ill.

Scorpio

This month, a rare opportunity to steer things onto the right path will fall into your lap. Take advantage, and don't waste any time!

Work. In August, you will be busier than ever at work, and many will be supporting you – friends, mentors, and loved ones. With that help, you will be able to resolve many important, difficult tasks, which have been keeping you up at night for quite some time. They will involve your relationship with certain hostile partners, who have been acting like adversaries for some time. You can expect open conflict with them during the first ten days of the month, but thanks to favorable circumstances, you will be able to mitigate the situation, and possibly even resolve it, for once and for all.

Your relationship with colleagues from other cities or abroad is moving along successfully, and if you are planning a move to launch your own business in another city or abroad, you will take important steps toward turning that idea into a reality. Entrepreneurs will acquire real estate for further developing their business, while employees will make arrangements to go somewhere new, if they have decided to take their work somewhere far away.

Money. Moneywise, things will be quiet for you in August. You will be receiving money regularly, and slightly more of it. Expect to receive the largest sums on August 7-8, 15-17, and 20-22.

Love and family. Your personal life is on the back burner this month – work comes first! But those who, by the will of fate, work exclusively at home and with their family, will continue to grapple with problems from last month.

Your relationship with your relatives is even and harmonious, and some family members may help you get out of a tricky situation related to a rigid spouse, in cases involving those who have been in a protracted war.

This time, your friends or family members may act as intermediaries, who will help you resolve thorny issues. They will succeed, at least partially.

Stable couples will manage with the help of influential friends and even family members, when it comes to completing important tasks related to a move or setting up somewhere new.

August is not a bad month for couples, whose relationship will grow stronger. You may take a trip together, and see friends and relatives who live in other cities or abroad.

Health. This month, you are healthy, energetic, and feel like you can move mountains. Do whatever you feel you need to do – this is your time!

Sagittarius

August is a dynamic, positive month for you, despite the fact that you still need a detailed plan of action. That will help you avoid mistakes and better take advantage of the opportunities handed to you by fate.

Work. In all areas, late August and September are the best times at work for any professional events. During the first ten days of the month, however, many Sagittarians will face a series of problems, which began long ago. They will involve tricky situations with colleagues from other cities or abroad, procrastination with red tape, documentation, and, potentially, the laws of other countries. You work doggedly though, and will see results – during the second half of the month, some of your problems will be resolved in your favor, and things will be charging ahead.

The second half of the month, entrepreneurs and managers will begin new projects, and also receive profits from some of their past work.

Many will receive tempting offers, which will take their work to the next level, or perhaps bring a new job, with an attractive salary.

At the very end of the month, you will reconnect with old friends, and they may have a positive influence on all of your work, this month.

Money. Financially speaking, August will be one of the best months this year. You will regularly have money coming in, and it will be significantly more than usual. You can expect the largest sums on August 1, 9, 10, 17-19, and 27-29. Your expenses are low, and within your means.

Love and family. Your personal life might take up much less attention than work, these days. Those who, at the will of fate or due to other obligations, spend their time at home taking care of their family, will face problems involving close relatives during the first ten days of the month. The situation might look differently, depending on your past. In some cases, this will involve old arguments, while in others, it will revolve around trouble your relatives have been facing for some time.

Spouses and couples will have an ordinary month; you are not expected to face any changes, but you might not have much time to spend together, due to how busy you are in other areas of your life.

Health. This month, you are bounding with energy, and you are not likely to fall ill. During the first ten days of the month, however, be careful while traveling or driving. there is a very high likelihood of accidents, injuries, and other unpleasant incidents during this period.

Capricorn

Traditionally, August is not the best time of the year for you. The situations you will encounter this month will strongly remind you of everything you went through in the recent past. That will help you cope, and possibly even resolve your task.

Work. During the first ten days of August, you will start actively expanding your business, and, most likely, that will take place in another city or abroad. You may have plans related to setting up another business for this purpose.

Your relationship with colleagues out of town or abroad is moving along very well, and this will become most apparent between August 11 and 20, as well as all of September. You might take a trip, which will be highly successful, especially if you have a detailed plan in hand, and a well-developed project.

Money. Financially, the first ten days of August will be the most difficult. During this time, for various reasons, you will end up spending large amounts of money. In some cases, the expenses may be related to business development, while in others, they will stem from your family's needs, particularly those of your children.

Love and family. Your personal life is looking tumultuous and stressful during the first ten days of the month. Once again, parents will have to deal with problems involving their children, which will lead to major expenses. In some cases, you will have to make painful decisions related to your children's affairs, and in others, you will simply have to put up the funds for their education, training, and development.

This is also a difficult time for couples. You may have unexpected arguments, for various reasons, or end up spending some time apart. During the second half of the month, however, you will reach a compromise, and it is very likely that you will go on a trip. The second half of the month, as well as all of September, is a great time for you to get clarity on both personal and professional matters, while significantly improving them, as well.

Health. You are not particularly energetic in August, and many Capricorns might not feel particularly confident or cheerful. Those who are elderly or weak should be particularly vigilant, as should those suffering from chronic heart or spinal disease. The last ten days of the month are looking much calmer, as the stars will be on your side for everything, including your health.

Aquarius

"Bad peace is better than a good fight" is an excellent proverb to keep in mind, all month. You can reach a compromise – both at work and when it comes to love.

Work. During the first ten days of August, you will, once again, deal with complaints from associates, who have their eyes on a large part of your property. Real estate or other property is on the agenda, but this time, you can expect any disputes to take a positive turn. During the second half of the month, it will be clear that compromise is indeed a possibility, and all you need is to give something up to your adversaries.

Most likely, that is the direction you will take, and you will not have to wait long for a peace agreement. This time, the problem may be nearly resolved, which means that by next month, you would already have the documents in your hand. You and your adversaries will both make concessions – and your longstanding dispute will finally come to an end. Don't give up your main position, though, as in the end, things will turn out in your favor!

Money. Financially, August will bring a lot of ups and downs. During the first ten days of the month, your income will be low, and you might end up with an empty wallet. But just wait a little bit, as for the rest of the month, you may see money coming in from real estate transactions, as well as debt repayments from both adversaries and associates.

Love and family. In many cases, your problems in August will revolve around family matters. At the beginning of the month, couples on the rocks will feel that they have once again come right back to where they started. But that is not the case – your conflict has run out of steam, and it may be that both sides now realize that there is no point in continuing. With time, you will have some decisions to make, if you want to avoid a stalemate.

Stable couples might fight for their own home or other real estate together, but things are now reaching their final stage, which is a positive development.

In many families, problems will continue with parents, and they will look differently, depending on past situations. Things will be resolved soon, and during the second half of the month, or the first ten days of September, that will become clear.

Health. This month, your energy levels are not particularly high, and you will have to get some good sleep and spend some time in nature on the weekends in order to get your strength back.

Pisces

August will bring with it difficult tests, which, fortunately, may be the last. You can expect the seas to be less stormy soon.

Work. The first ten days of August will be the most difficult period of the month. During this time, you can expect old legal problems to rear their heads again, hostility from colleagues in other cities or abroad, and negative or deliberately mischaracterized information.

During the second half of August, and close to the end of the month, the situation may be resolved. You might see help from benevolent business partners, influential members of society, or even a friend. Their efforts will not be in vain, and in late August or September, you can expect to clear your schedule of any of the stressors bothering you now. This is also the case for those dealing with dragged out investigations. Entrepreneurs should keep an eye on their subordinates, and employees should be careful with colleagues. There is a high likelihood of conflict from August 1 to 10.

Money. Financially, August is tumultuous. You will not receive much income, but your expenses will be reasonable, too. You can expect to receive the largest sums on August 7, 8, 16, 17, and 25-27.

Love and family. You can also expect old problems to resurface in your personal life. During the first ten days of the month, many Pisces will deal with hostile relatives, and this is not the first time. Nonetheless, your spouse or loved one will help you get through this, and, in the end, things will fall into place. You will not have to wait long to find common ground with your rebellious family member.

If your loved ones are facing problems that have lasted nearly a year, the time will come when your joint efforts will lead to a favorable resolution.

Spouses' relationships will be harmonious, and the person closest to you will be a support during difficult times.

Health. Those who are happily spared personal or professional problems might see their health suffer instead. The first ten days of the month are the most dangerous time, when you are extremely likely to see old, chronic conditions return, or an unexpected appearance of new health issues. During this inauspicious period, the stars recommend that drivers and travelers take extra care – there is also a high probability of accidents and other unfortunate incidents.

September

Aries

In September, you will have to prove that you are capable of completing jobs assigned to you. This is the only way to open the door to a better future.

Work. As far as work is concerned, September is fairly positive. Entrepreneurs and managers will be able to promote a major project and earn some decent money. Your team of subordinates is now working efficiently and harmoniously, but small disagreements are highly likely during the first part of the month, though they will not reflect on your workflow.

You will connect with old friends, and influential mentors as well, which will add another ray of light to September's sunny outlook.

The astrologer recommends planning your most important tasks and meetings for the first 20 days of September. The last week of the month, and nearly all of October, you can expect strong influence from Mercury in retrograde. That means that your partners may stall meetings, fail to fulfill obligations on time, or simply not show up.

Money. Financially, September will be a good month for you. You will regularly receive money, and significantly more of it. You can expect to receive the largest amounts on September 6, 7, 15, 16, and 24-26.

Your expenses will be reasonable, predictable, and modest.

Love and family. Your personal life might temporarily be less of a priority while you are busy dealing with work and money issues. In order to not lose touch with your loved ones and not miss anything important, try to be more attentive and remember that some kind words and a smile can nip a lot of problems in the bud.

This advice is particularly relevant during the second half of September, when you begin to see cracks in your relationships. Remember that things may get much worse in October, and act accordingly. This is very important for spouses and couples.

Health. This month, you are feeling energetic and are not at risk of any illness. Many Aries will want to work on improving their appearance and wardrobe or lose weight after some turbulent years. The stars are giving you the green light and promise excellent results.

Taurus

This month, you can expect a lot – victory at work and success on the personal front. It seems that the clouds are clearing on the horizon.

Work. You are on a positive streak at work – important, positive changes are underway. Employees may see a promotion at their current job, or perhaps a new and interesting job elsewhere. Entrepreneurs will begin new projects and dusting off those that had been shelved earlier.

Negotiations with the powers that be during the first half of the month will turn out very favorable. But this is just a first, albeit very important step. After September 25, you will begin the second phase, and things will get longer and more complicated. In the end, though, you will be sure to achieve that you set out to do, and the stars strongly urge you to boost your position in negotiations with paperwork and documentation – the second phase will run much more smoothly.

Your communication with associates from other cities or abroad is becoming dynamic, and during the first ten days of the month, you may go on a trip, which will turn out very successfully.

Money. Financially speaking, September looks somewhat neutral. You will not end up penniless, and money will come in regularly, in the same amounts you initially expected.

You will receive the largest sums of money on September 8, 9, 17, 18, and 26-28.

Love and family. This month, many Taureans will be juggling work, family, and romance.

Married couples will spend time with their children, and may go on a trip together. Couples will break their routine, and may also spend some time somewhere far away from home. Whether you go to the countryside or the Bahamas, you are guaranteed to enjoy yourselves.

Many will also see their loved ones who live in other cities or abroad.

Health. This month, you are feeling healthy, energized, and very attractive – everyone fate puts in your path will notice, too.

Gemini

"There's no place like home" and "my home is my castle" are your mottos in September.

Work. September is a time for putting your finances in order and getting organized. This is what entrepreneurs and managers are doing, if they plan to open their own business, and in some cases, that will be in another city or abroad.

Various problems and stressors from the past seem to be resolved, now, and you can now dedicate all of your efforts to the work at hand, which bodes well for the future.

You will reconnect with long-term associates from other cities or abroad, and you might have productive meetings or favorable negotiations, too.

Employees will take a short trip somewhere and focus on family or home, which is especially relevant if you are moving somewhere new.

All changes at work are clearly for the better. You are beginning a new chapter, and it promises to be a successful one!

Money. Your financial situation is stable, but most of your money will come from such as sponsorship, credit, and support from parents or a loved one. You may also receive profits from various real estate transactions, whether from sales or rent.

Love and family. Many Geminis will find that September is a time for getting their personal affairs in order. You are likely to change your living space – repairing or buying an apartment, home, or perhaps something else related to home improvement.

In all cases, this month you are likely to see strong influence from your parents and elder family members, especially your mother. In addition to moral support, you might count on material help as well.

Parents will focus on their children's future, and might spend a lot of time on their development and education. You are likely to see some problems in this area toward the end of the month, and in October, as well.

September is a good month for couples, as well. After sleepless nights and worries, they might decide to live together, and in some cases, to get married.

The first half of September is the best time for both personal and professional events.

The last ten days of September will be less dynamic, as your ruler, Mercury, will move into retrograde after September 27. That means that you can expect setbacks at work, and various problems. This period will continue until October 18, so it is worth tackling any important tasks during the first 20 days of the month.

Health. In September, you are feeling somewhat sluggish, but if you watch your schedule, you will be able to avoid any problems You might find yourself gaining weight, so don't forget to exercise and watch your diet.

Cancer

In September, you can finally give a sigh of relief – your problems are now over. You can now choose your future, depending on your own wishes and desires.

Work. Most Cancers in the work force will find their positions stronger in September, and that their ties with colleagues from other cities or abroad are becoming more important.

Many are laying the groundwork for a move, opening their own business somewhere far away from home, and they may now be preparing events related to that.

Your plans will become more specific a little later on – in 2022. But right now, you are in reconnaissance mode. September is still a time to make new acquaintances and find new friends. If you meet someone during the last ten days of the month, you should keep a healthy skepticism. Not everyone is reliable, but only time will tell.

As you are making new connections, follow your own intuition. It rarely fails you, as long as you are able to listen to it.

Any trips planned for the first twenty days of September will turn out very successfully.

Closer to the end of the month, you will have to grapple with economic and organizational tasks, which will continue into October.

Money. Your financial situation is most likely neutral in September. You are not expected to see any changes.

Love and family. Your personal life is also looking more even and positive. Bitter spouses are able to resolve matters related to real estate, and most likely, not have to come back to them again. If the situation does repeat itself, then it will not be as challenging as it has been.

Stable couples will go on a trip, which may shed light on their future.

Some will think about moving to another city or abroad, and begin taking their first steps in that direction. In any case, the astrologist believes that this decision will not be resolved until 2022.

Your relationship with relatives will become significantly more dynamic, and you might take a trip to see family living in other cities or abroad.

September will be kind to single people. Your social circle will expand, and most likely, that will take place while you are traveling or among people who have come from afar. You might also have an interesting encounter or romance, which might add a splash of color to your life, even if it doesn't last for long.

Health. In September, you are healthy, energetic, and feel ready to move mountains. But you won't need it- the mountains will happily move for you, this time.

Leo

You will feel confident in your efforts all month, and you have plenty of reasons for that!

Work. Professionally speaking, this month is one of your best in 2021. No matter what you are dealing with, you will see quick success.

Entrepreneurs are starting new business, and will also see profits from a previous project.

Employees might count on a raise this month, and in the best-case scenario, a job with a new, promising organization.

Old arguments with associates, legal problems, and other troubles are a thing of the past, and now, you have time to work on building a new future.

You are slowly reconnecting with previous associates, and most likely, they are colleagues from another city or abroad. During the first ten days of the month, you might begin negotiations, which will lead to positive results in the near future.

Try to finish all your important tasks and meetings by September 26 or 27, as Mercury will be in retrograde after that, and, most of the time, that means that everything will suddenly slow down.

Money. September might be one of the best months of 2021 when it comes to your finances. Money is coming in regularly, and there is significantly more of it. You can expect to receive the largest amounts on September 5-7, 14-16, and 24-26. Your expenses are low, predictable, and reasonable.

Love and family. Your personal life is currently on the back burner – work and money come first! But those who spend their days at home can count on a much better relationship with your loved ones.

If your marriage has been on the rocks, you might find that dedicated relatives are able to persuade you to reconcile. September may have fateful significance for couples; conflicts with parents are now a thing of the past, and you might make a decision about marriage or living arrangements.

Health. This September you are feeling healthy, energetic, confident, and that is a good sign that you have no reason to fear any illnesses. It is worth mentioning that the first twenty days of the month are a great time for shopping, changing your look, and other cosmetic procedures.

Virgo

September is a colorful, positive month for you, and you will be able to tackle any task and manage it skillfully. The stars are definitely on your side, now!

Work. It seems that your recent, longstanding problems are finally behind you. Your rocky relationship with colleagues from other cities or countries is now on steady footing, thanks to your efforts. You might go on a trip, have successful negotiations, or start a potential cooperation.

Despite the favorable tides, overall, given the state of affairs, you should closely monitor everything happening, as so much of it depends on you, and you alone.

You are very interested in continuing some projects, but your partners are less so. Keep this in mind, and act accordingly.

On the other hand, you also have reliable, conscientious, and responsible colleagues and assistance. Their help in everything you do this month might end up being truly priceless.

Employees will strengthen their position at work, and may continue to receive additional responsibilities. The stars believe this will prove to be very beneficial.

In other cases, you might be thinking about a new job, and an offer from colleagues in other cities or abroad.

Money. Your financial situation is largely stable now. That was not the case for a long time, but now, things are looking good. You will regularly have money coming in, and there will be a lot more of it. You can expect the largest sums on September 8-9, 17, 18, and 26-28.

Love and family. You may see some minor problems in your personal life. Spouses or loved ones might not be particularly excited over your undertakings at work, and that may lead to misunderstandings and conflict.

This is the best time for single people and those who have been let down by love in the past. More likely than not, you will meet someone new this month. You might meet them on a trip, or among people who have come from far away.

Even if the relationship starts out casually, with time, it will become clear there is more to it. You don't always feel an immediate spark, so don't rush things, you have the whole year ahead of you!

Your relationship with your children will grow stronger, especially if they are already grown, including if they live in other cities or abroad.

Trips planned for September will be very successful.

Health. This month, you are feeling energetic and healthy, and you are able to exert major influence over anything fate throws your way.

Libra

The heavens will give you a real gift in September. If you are drawn to leisure and entertainment, give in to your desires. You are worth it, and you definitely deserve it.

Work. Though you might consider September a month for focusing on home, hopeless workaholics will still be able to get their work done. Both entrepreneurs and managers will work on administrative matters, getting the office in order, production facilities, and their teams. The latter is particularly important, as there is still someone untrustworthy in the ranks.

Soon, you will likely find the people you need, but for now, keep a close eye on the situation, check up on your associates, and follow up on anything relevant.

If you work in construction or your business is somehow related to real estate and land, things are about to get complicated. You will have to work to carry out everything you had planned and dreamed about.

Money. Your financial situation is sustainable in September. Business is going well for your spouse and parents, which is having a positive impact on the whole family budget. It is highly likely you will see profits from successful real estate transactions, as well. Expenses for your children are much lower, now, though they are unlikely to completely disappear.

Love and family. Many Libras are spending most of their time with their family in September. You may see big changes at home – repairs, acquiring new furniture, and appliances, or décor come to mind. In many cases, these changes are planned in order to resolve matters related to your children. Things are going much better for them, but you have not reached stability quite yet. But the progress is palpable, and there is hope that in the near future this painful part of your life will be healed.

The first ten days of September are favorable to couples. During this time, you might reconcile, if your relationship recently fell apart over arguments. Remember that very soon the stars will stop putting the strength of your feelings to the test and be patient.

Health. This month, many Libras will be spending some time on themselves, their health, their appearance, and wardrobe. This is a good time for you to spend a week or two at a health resort or to simply spend a weekend in nature.

Scorpio

This month, you're saying goodbye to the past and starting over. Right now, connections will resolve everything!

Work. The positive steps that began last month are continuing in September. With the help of intermediaries – possibly old friends or superiors, you will be able to resolve your underlying problems with stubborn foes. That means that the door to the future is wide open!

Your connections to colleagues from other cities or abroad will become very important, and those planning to expand their business somewhere far away might count on significant assistance with promoting their projects.

During the first ten days of September, you might see new people on your horizon, though not all of them are reliable or trustworthy. Don't rush things, and check out your new acquaintances, as well as their invitations, in order to avoid disappointment in the future.

During the last ten days of the month, many Scorpios will have to deal with economic and administrative tasks. That is particularly relevant for those who are busy launching a business in another city or abroad.

Money. Financially speaking, September is likely to be neutral. Your income is not high, and most of it is related to support from business partners, as well as various real estate transactions.

Those who are outside of the business world might count on help from their spouse, a loved one, parents, or elder relatives.

Love and family. You can't avoid changes in your family life, but this time, they are looking positive. Couples who recently survived a crisis might find a path toward reconciliation, and friends, relatives, or mutual acquaintances will help you.

If you are in the process of splitting up for good, you will find an acceptable compromise. But you may have to deal with dividing up joint property, most likely real estate.

Those moving somewhere far away might have to amicably resolve matters related to making arrangements somewhere new, and that process will continue until October.

The shared influence of the Sun, Uranus, and Mars will be favorable to single people. New, unusual, and interesting people are on their horizon. That may include a new friend, a neighbor, or a fellow traveler. Basically- you don't have to look very far, happiness will come to you!

Health. This month, you are feeling energetic enough, and you are not likely to fall ill. If you want to change something about yourself, for example, updating your wardrobe or a new hairstyle, the first week of September is the best week to do it!

Sagittarius

The movements of the stars in the sky promise you many things – above all, business success! Don't just rest on your laurels – the stakes are high, now!

Work. Professionally speaking, September is one of the best months of the year for you. You are likely to receive new, tempting invitations, which may come from associates from other cities or abroad this time.

You have an excellent chance of getting a new, attractive job somewhere new, or carrying out appealing projects, whether you are an employee or entrepreneur.

Friends or highly-placed mentors may play an important role in all areas of business this month. Their help will be priceless with anything that is related to resolving previous problems, as well as promoting new projects.

For any work-related events, the most successful period will be the first twenty days of September. During the last ten days, things will slow down significantly, and that situation is expected to continue into October. Therefore, it is best to knock on doors between September 1 and 20, one of them is sure to open.

Trips planned for this period will turn out to be very productive, and you will meet many new people.

Money. Financially speaking, September is one of the best months of 2021. Money will be coming in regularly, and there will be a lot more of it, too. You can expect to receive the largest amounts on September 6-8, 14-16, and 24-26.

Your expenses are low, predictable, and reasonable.

Love and family. Your personal life will be relegated to the back burner, so long as you are focused on work. This is a temporary situation, though, in a few months, you will be very busy with personal matters.

Right now, spouses may find themselves spending some time apart, but for purely objective reasons. In order to avoid any misunderstandings or offense, explain to your loved ones why you are so busy, and that you are not only working for your own benefit. That goes for unmarried couples, too.

Single people have an excellent chance of finding their destiny, and in many cases, that will happen while traveling or among people who have come from afar.

Those moving somewhere far away might be busy with various tasks related to setting up a new household, in addition to work. They are only taking their first steps in that direction right now; you can expect greater progress closer to 2022.

Health. In September, you are feeling energetic, charming, and sharp, and that is the first sign that any illnesses are now in the past.

Capricorn

Sometimes, there comes a time when you need to make serious changes in certain areas of your life. September is one of those times. Onward!

Work. This month, you are unlikely to spend much time sitting at home – you have travel, meetings, and business to take care of, and that is your theme, all month long.

Entrepreneurs will link their plans to colleagues from far away, and spare no efforts in reaching their cherished goals.

It is possible that all the movement in September will be preliminary in nature, and the main events are for later on. They will focus on developing your business in another city or abroad. In many cases, September's agreements will be directly related to these planned changes.

During the first twenty days of the month, you are on a quite favorable streak, which applies to all Capricorns, regardless of where they work. Employees will strengthen their position at work this month, or receive new, attractive offers.

Entrepreneurs can count on unexpected deals and profits from previous work.

During the last ten days of the month, things will be less exciting, and that will be noticeable closer to the end of the month. For that reason, you should try to schedule major events and meetings for the first twenty days of September.

Money. Financially speaking, this month is not bad at all. You will be receiving money regularly, and slightly more of it, too. You can expect to receive the largest sums of money on September 8-19, 17-18, 26, and 28. Your expenses are minimal, and in any case, they are often for pleasure, rather than necessity.

Love and family. Your personal life is also going through positive changes. Situations involving children will improve greatly, and you will have to find a common ground with them this month. In some cases, you will find a shared cause, and in others, you will find a way to relax or otherwise spend time having fun together It seems that the stars will stop testing your strength in this very important area of your life.

Spouses will not be particularly joyful this month, but you also won't find sadness. Things might be best for unmarried couples – you might find your feelings are suddenly much stronger; even if you recently separated due to an argument, you will be able to find a path to each other's hearts. You might go on a trip together, which will help strengthen the relationship.

Single people and those who have been disappointed by past partners are in for a real surprise – an unexpected meeting, a lively romance, which will add some excitement to your life, even if it does not last for long.

Health. Many Capricorns will get a surge of energy, another gift during what will be a wonderful month.

Aquarius

September is a favorable month for you. You will see major changes, which you spent a long time fighting for, and now, they are actually happening. Buckle up!

Work. For most Aquarians, September is a time for economic or administrative tasks. You might see a positive resolution to longstanding, difficult issues related to land, real estate, or other large assets belonging to your business. Even if you have to struggle a bit, most of the work will be done in September.

Your relationship with colleagues from other cities or abroad is moving along nicely, and you will receive good news or go on a productive trip during the first half of the month.

Those who work in construction, or whose business is somehow related to real estate will be particularly successful this month.

For most of September, employees will be busy with personal or family matters, though you are not expected to run into any problems there. Some may be successful here and there, and some may go on vacation for a week or two.

The first twenty days of the month are the best time for any professional activities. During the last ten days, Mercury will be in retrograde, which will slow everything down, and even lead to delays in many cases. This is particularly relevant for any work involving documents, as well as that with colleagues from afar.

Money. Moneywise, September is fairly calm, but that is about it. The exception is those working in construction, and anyone whose business is somehow related to real estate – business is booming, and your profits will rise.

However, those who want to buy or rent an apartment, home, or cottage might also be able to count on September's positive influence and use it to their advantage.

Love and family. Many Aquarians are fully immersed in family and personal affairs in September. You might be busy ending longstanding disputes related to property, particularly real estate.

Stable couples might come to a favorable resolution of a delicate issue related to their home, involving scammers or construction companies.

Hostile spouses will be able to find a way out of an unpleasant situation involving real estate, particularly their own home.

This is the month when many will resolve matters related to their residence which have troubled them for some time. If some of the issues have been discussed already, the main problems are already resolved, and there is no turning back, now.

Many will resolve various problems involving their parents, and they may even receive some help from them. You might receive an inheritance from older family members.

Health. In September, many Aquarians will feel less than cheerful and confident. On the contrary, you are susceptible to fatigue and tiredness, but living a healthy lifestyle and spending time in nature can help. If you have a tendency to gain weight, which is highly likely in September, consider eating a balanced diet.

Pisces

In September, do not make any decisions until you have asked those around you for their opinion. It is better to work as part of a team – keep that in mind and don't try to make it all about you.

Work. September is a good time for meetings negotiations, and signing contracts. In all issues that have been bothering you, you are able to count on the support of associates, friends, or influential mentors. Thanks to their help, you are able to favorably resolve longstanding legal issues, handle any audits, and also establish good relations with colleagues from afar. Here, it all depends on where you are having trouble.

You will still need a few months before you are able to put a painful period at work behind you, but the main developments are happening right now.

For anything work-related, the first twenty days of September are the best time, as this is when conversations on anything that is troubling you will be extremely successful.

During the last ten days of the month, you will begin conversations on financial matters, and this will continue into October.

The first twenty days of October are a good time for those involved in the creative professions – actors, artists, and musicians. You will have the public's attention, and if you are planning a tour, it will be a smashing success.

Money. Your finances are likely to be neutral in September. You might receive support from your business partners, and it might be moral as well as financial. Those who are not part of the business world can count on help from their loved ones.

Love and family. Family issues, as well as new information about a loved one, will take up most of your energy during the first half of September. This is most relevant with regards to your relationship with relatives, which are under pressure from the heavens throughout 2021. This time, everything is different – and your spouse or someone close to you is likely to play a major role in mitigating things. Their efforts are not in vain – a conflict from someone stubborn is slowly fading away, and in the future, you will support this process. By 2022, your relationship will be calm and peaceful.

Stable couples will continue to work on home improvement projects, and, the astrologist believes, this process will move closer to a favorable ending.

September is a great time for single people, who may have unexpected encounters, an exciting romance which turns into something interesting, with a traditional ending – a marriage proposal – though the last part will have to wait until 2022.

Health. In September, you are not particularly energetic, and that will be most noticeable toward the end of the month. The astrologist believes that the best way to gain your strength is by staying busy, trying to get enough sleep, and avoiding any gossip.

October

Aries

Your diplomatic talents will come in handy in October. You will have to adapt to your surroundings and find out who your real friends and enemies are.

Work. After a dynamic, productive September, October might seem like a bit of a letdown. Your negotiations with partners are stalling for various reasons. You may need to discuss financial terms for future cooperation, and that may not always be easy.

Friends or benevolent mentors and superiors may help you with this or other issues, and they will have a clearly positive influence this month.

The stars suggest that you stick to your plans, but you should be flexible enough, and never rush things. Everything will turn out almost as you had planned, just a little later – near the end of October, or November. In some areas, you will have to reach a compromise.

You are connecting well with colleagues from afar, and the results will pay off in dividends in the near future.

Employees will face competition in October, but it is not worth arguing with management, unless there are special circumstances. In case of any problems, your friends or someone higher up in the organization might help you.

Money. Your financial situation this month is neutral, but in the near future, the stars promise much more. You can expect the largest sums of money to come in on October 12, 13, 21, 22, and 31.

Love and family. Your personal life is very much up and down right now. Someone close to you might go from one extreme to another, and occasionally behave erratically or inappropriately. You will have nothing left to do, once you adapt to their mood. Try to be flexible during this difficult period, and don't get hung up on things. Most likely, it is nothing serious. This is a temporary misunderstanding, and nothing more. This advice is equally relevant for married and unmarried couples.

Young people are likely to fight with their parents, and the problem may be money or other material things.

Health. This month, your energy is lagging, and that is most noticeable in late October. During the last days of the month, take care of yourself, and avoid any fall colds and infections. Take care of any chronic illnesses, as well.

Taurus

October is a good time for taking stock of things and tying up loose ends. Think things through, plan them out, and don't rush anything. There is no need for that.

Work. This month, you will have to resolve some problems that have been giving you trouble for some time. To do that, you will need to take care of some paperwork and red tape, and discuss the terms for concluding old business. This will be long and challenging.

In other cases, you might have long conversations about new projects or jobs. Whatever you do right now will strongly determine the future, so be careful and take time to really study things, without rushing them. Your relationship with colleagues in other cities or abroad will also get on the right track, and you might once again strike an agreement with them.

The last ten days of October is the best time for any work-related events. Work will be slow, but you will see progress. During this time, the stars recommend that you listen to your partners' suggestions and avoid any confrontation. You can do this – believe in yourself!

Money. Your financial situation is looking stable, and you will not see any problems or excess here. You can expect to receive the largest amounts on October 6, 7, 14, 15, and 23-25.

Love and family. Your personal life might not seem terribly exciting, right now, since you're so busy with work. But if you are in a peaceful mood, then your partner will be, too. That goes for stable couples, as well as for those going through a period of difficulties and marriage.

Right now, bad peace is better than a good fight. Keep that in mind, and act accordingly.

Health. This month, you will be feeling more run-down than usual, and you might feel less than confident and cheerful.

Right now is the time to quit any bad habits, follow a balanced diet, and think about other ways to live a healthy lifestyle. Remember that a healthy mind lives in a healthy body, and act accordingly.

Gemini

It's time to pay attention to what is happening around you. Be sensitive to your partner, and you will be pleasantly surprised with the results.

Work. Even if many Geminis see big changes in their personal and romantic lives this month, incorrigible workaholics will still be able to achieve a lot at work.

You can improve your relationship with colleagues in other cities or abroad, work on legal issues, and also get any necessary paperwork in order.

This is how the first twenty days of October will play out. During the last ten days, things will become more dynamic, as well as challenging. You will have to grapple with difficult issues related to promoting new projects or holding delicate negotiations for a new job.

Many Geminis will be able to overcome these challenges related to opening a new business somewhere far away, or perhaps legal issues, the laws in another country, or partners' reticence to meeting you halfway.

Money. Expect financial instability in October. During the first twenty days of the month, you will have expenses related to your children, loved ones, or home improvement.

You can count on some money on October 1, 16, 17, 26, and 27.

Love and family. Many events will be related to your personal life in October. Parents will spend time with their children, who will require your attention and care. It's possible that their needs will also involve a large part of your family's budget.

Couples might see their dreams come true, and this may involve marriage. Much of October will be devoted to this major issue.

It seems that everything is going well, but at some point, you will begin to have doubts again. It is not worth sharing these thoughts with your partner, as any doubts and hesitation are your problem, not theirs. Work on these matters on your own, before acting.

Those who are moving somewhere far away will have to deal with issues related to setting up their home, their children's future, and will find themselves very busy with these bothersome tasks.

Health. This month, you are healthy and energetic, but also stressed and anxious. In this case, be sure to get enough sleep, and get regular meals.

Cancer

In October, the best place for you is your own home, with your loved ones. There's no place like home, and that is all you need, right now.

Work. October is not a very promising month at work, unless you work in construction or your business is somehow related to real estate or land. In that case, you will have to finish up projects, file paperwork, or deal with other, irritating administrative tasks.

Managers or entrepreneurs may also be busy with administrative tasks.

An old feud with associates is also approaching its end. You might have conversations about various issues related to property, and the paperwork that goes with it.

The stars recommend carefully studying documents and keep an eye on the details, too. After October 18, Mercury will be in retrograde, so mistakes are highly likely. If you see that things are playing out more slowly than you would like, don't worry – you have an excellent opportunity to double-check everything.

Money. Your financial situation is looking calm. You may see profit from successful real estate transactions, whether a sale or rent. You are highly likely to see financial support from a loved one – parents or a spouse. You won't end up broke, which is the most important thing, right now.

Love and family. Many Cancers will spend October occupied with home and family. You might be busy with repairs, acquiring appliances, or décor, and the likeliest possibility is selling an old home and planning on buying a new one.

Divorcing or divorced couples are finally dealing with property issues, and might finally put any disagreements behind them.

Parents will only have positive influence in their children's affairs. You might get major assistance with setting up or buying a home.

Health. This month, you are not particularly energetic, and you might often feel tired, fatigued, and unwilling to move. You may gain weight as a result.

The stars recommend you begin your day with a cup of coffee, which will wake up your body and mind.

Leo

This month, you are jumping through some final hoops, which will have a positive effect on your work. Remember to follow your plan, and don't let the details pass you by.

Work. Entrepreneurs and managers will hold negotiations with partners in October, with varying success. Some will be slower than you had anticipated.

Work-related and administrative issues may become a stumbling block, and you will have to discuss them and deal with red tape. You might hold long consultations with attorneys, who will painstakingly pore over any legally required documents. This time, everything will take place peacefully, as both parties are tired of fighting.

The stars recommend being cautious and careful when looking over any documents required for work, as Mercury will be in retrograde from October 1 to 18. That means that any mistakes in important paperwork are highly likely. You are also likely to come across incorrect or deliberately twisted information.

This advice is also relevant for anyone planning on cooperating with colleagues from other cities or abroad. All month, remember the phrase, "trust but verify!"

Money. Your financial situation is looking uncertain this month. You might see money held up until the end of the month, when things will finally change. But that only applies to what you expect to come in, and you might also see money on October 3, 4, and 31.

Love and family. You are spending a lot of time with your relatives this month. These family ties might help you through a disagreement with your partner. If your loved one is having problems, then you can count on support from your own family.

If you have recently had a major argument or divorced, your relatives might help you deal with major issues involving property, and in case you and your partner are able to find common ground, assist with your reconciliation.

In the worst-case scenario, you will have to turn to a qualified attorney for help.

With help from relatives, couples will be able to overcome resistance from their parents, and you can expect to get married or move in together, soon.

Health. You are feeling healthy in October, especially if you are experiencing less stress, gossip, and getting to bed on time.

Virgo

October is a beautiful fall month, but you can expect to deal with a lot of trouble and running around. Fortunately, there aren't many bumps in the road, but there also won't be any outside help. Basically – things will be the same as always.

Work. For most Virgos, money is number one in October. No matter what field you work in, you will have conversations about money all month long, and this includes both entrepreneurs and employees.

Decisions as to who owes how much to whom, and who owns what may drag out, until all sides reach a reasonable solution, which will not be easy.

Despite the holdups, a peaceful, acceptable ending is possible. The stars recommend that you refrain from trying to make it all about you, and you respect others' interests. If you manage this, the outcome will be better.

In all cases, managers will be able to count on their subordinates this month, and employees on their colleagues.

Your relationship with colleagues from other cities or abroad is moving forward with varying success – some things are working out, and others less so. But this is a natural process, and soft skills are important when promoting and following your side of things. This is particularly important closer to the end of October and November.

Money. Most of the month, you will be focused on money – and not in vain! You will receive money regularly, and significantly more of it than usual. You can expect the most, in increasingly large amounts, to come in on October 6, 7, 14, 15, and 23-25.

You will also have some expenses, most of which will be related to your personal life and family needs – most of all, those of your children.

Love and family. Your personal life might seem less exciting than work, right now. Many couples are slowly and quietly heading toward a breakup or separation. Can you avoid that? Of course! But to do this, you will have to pay closer attention to your partner. If you do that, they will do the same for you, too.

Your relationship with your children will get slightly more complicated. You may be dealing with problems that have required attention, care, and serious financial investment for a while, now. Remember – "little kids, little problems. Big kids, big problems".

Health. For a while, now, you have had less energy than usual, and October is no exception. Saturn, which is responsible for health, and requires discipline, limits, and personal responsibility, is firmly settled in your sector of the sky. You have nothing to lose following these rules, but plenty to gain.

Libra

October will bring excellent opportunities for your life, and that of those around you. You will be able to influence events in a way others cannot.

Work. This month is very important for relationships with both associates and adversaries. You might have long negotiations, in which you will be able to consistently defend your position. The astrologist believes that this is the best way.

You may have to come back to the same issues multiple times, particularly from October 1 to 18. This is also a time for a lot of red tape, and be sure to not miss any details. Mercury will be in retrograde, and all kinds of errors are likely, so double-check your work.

Your relationship with colleagues from other cities or abroad is moving along nicely in the second part of the month, and you might better understand each other and easily resolve a delicate situation. Trips planned on this period are expected to be very productive as well.

Many Libras might once again find themselves discussing difficult, thorny matters related to land or real estate, and the results look encouraging.

Money. This month, your financial outlook is good – your income will grow, and your expenses will be somewhat smaller, and mostly related to your family and children. This time, you will have a better understanding of the situation, and it will not be as severe.

Love and family. Your personal life is turbulent and stressful. Your relationship with your children has slowly improved, which is the only positive thing you can say. It seems that you have done everything in your power to get this important aspect of your life back on track, and you have managed to largely succeed.

But those whose marriage is on the rocks might find themselves arguing a lot, and once again, the problem is large assets, possibly real estate. Mars is in your sign, which gives you the strength you need to stick to your guns.

Though that is a good thing at work, it might not be the best when it comes to delicate family and romantic relationships. Remember this and employ your soft skills to the best of your ability. If your partner does not understand subtleties, however, then let your behavior reflect what is really going on.

Single people and those who have been let down before by love might recall past partners and resurrect old romances.

Health. This month, you are feeling energetic, and the astrologist strongly recommends using your abilities only for peaceful purposes.

Scorpio

October is a quiet month for you, and moderately favorable. You will see opportunities to collect your energy for a big push forward. Right now, take care not to rush, and be sure to let the situation unfold.

Work. October is not a particularly promising month for you at work. The best you can do if you are a manager or entrepreneur is get your affairs in order, as well as any production facilities. This is especially important if you are launching a new business or setting up any necessary workspaces.

In other cases, this may take place in another city or abroad, which will complicate matters further. If that applies to you, you may have to deal with paperwork and red tape, as well as obstacles presented by other countries' laws.

Employees will be immersed in family matters this month, and the stars strongly recommend that you take a vacation or some time off, in order to avoid any unfortunate incidents at work.

Money. October is very stable, financially speaking. In addition to your usual earnings, you can expect support from partners or someone close to you. You may even see profits from various real estate transactions.

Love and family. Many Scorpios will find that the most important events in October take place at home.

Anyone moving somewhere far away might have to conclude important tasks related to setting up a new home. If you were not able to buy a house during the first half of the year, you will be able to this month.

For others, repairs, new furniture, and other major purchases or changes in décor are on the horizon. In all cases, this month you will see support from your parents or elder family members.

Divorced couples will be able to resolve difficult matters related to shared property, particularly their home.

Health. This month, you are not particularly energetic, and you might sometimes even feel tired and run-down.

Be very careful if you are elderly or weak, as there is a high likelihood of old, chronic illnesses getting worse. Be very careful behind the wheel, especially from October 15 to 25.

Sagittarius

Despite the fact that Mercury is in retrograde, you can expect a rather positive month ahead. You are sure to achieve your goals, if you keep a cool head and remember to be patient.

Work. This month, you will need support in order to make your ideas happen, and you are sure to find it. Your old friends and influential members of society will take part in your business, and facilitate your projects coming to life.

You might see more contact with colleagues in other cities or abroad, and you will see friends or mentors act as intermediaries. Your negotiations may end up dragging out, but that will not have an effect on the results, which will be very positive near the end of the month.

All month, and particularly from October 1 to 18, the stars recommend that you pay close attention to any documentation. Mercury will be in retrograde, so mistakes and misunderstandings are highly probable.

Any trips planned between October 1 and 18 might be postponed, but they will certainly happen.

This month, any trips planned or business launches in other cities or abroad may go a long way toward achieving your dreams. The most important thing is to find the right approach with people whose efforts will be invaluable to you.

Money. Your finances are looking very up and down this month. You will be spending constantly, and the stars strongly urge you to reconsider your expenses, which might be out of your means. You can count on some money coming in on October 3-5, 12, 30, and 31.

Love and family. October 7, gorgeous Venus is moving into your sign, which means that your romantic and family life is about to improve. Couples might go on a trip together, which will strengthen their relationship, and spouses will work together to solve major issues related to a move.

Your relationship with relatives is gradually improving, and you might see old friends playing a big part in that. You may change your point of view with regard to certain events of the past, and understand that bad peace is better than a good fight.

All Sagittarians should remember to avoid making any promises which will be hard to fulfill later on, and don't take on too much responsibility, whether moral or financial in nature. This is certainly a tendency you will have to fight off in October.

Health. This month, you are feeling energetic, and are not at risk of any disease.

Capricorn

In October, you will try to change the world, or at least your surroundings. And in much of this, you will succeed.

Work. This month, you are up to your neck in work. Change is on the horizon, and your main task in October is to be prepared for them. In order to do that, you should carry out a careful analysis of your business, and then implement any necessary adjustments.

You will make some decisions this month, and some later on, but as an excellent strategist, you are able to imagine the future, and might start taking your first steps in that direction.

Most likely, this will involve expanding your business, and in many cases, that will take place in another city or abroad. Though the biggest changes will not be until 2022, nothing is preventing you from laying the groundwork already. Your friends might be intermediaries between you and future colleagues.

Employees might see changes in leadership at their place of employment, though these changes are only to your benefit. In October, you might discuss a promotion at work, or significantly expanding your authority.

Money. Your financial outlook is stable, you are earning more, and spending less. You can expect to receive the largest sums of money on October 6, 7, 14, 15, 23-25, and 28.

Love and family. Your personal life is not your priority in October, but this is a good thing. Parents will be less worried about their children, and problems are gradually resolving themselves. There is also hope that this positive process will continue in the future.

It is hard to predict the outlook for couples, but if you are already together, then that's already a good thing. Is there hope for a happy ending? Of course, there is! Let your relationship develop in its own way, and don't be afraid to take the first step.

Health. In October, you are healthy, attentive, and energetic. In a word, you feel ready to move mountains. Your enthusiasm is so contagious, though, that you won't have to – the mountains will move themselves.

Aquarius

This month, no one will find fault with your ambitions – you are doing a lot in the interest of achieving your goals, and finding a lot of success. Gradually, you are forging a path ahead to a respectable future.

Work. For most of October, you may find yourself discussing controversial issues with associates and adversaries. It will be very difficult to find common ground, and someone will have to argue, someone will have to say no, and several times, you will have to tackle paperwork and required documents. You may find yourself coming back to issues resolved long ago.

This is relevant for those who work with colleagues in other cities or abroad, as well as those who are struggling with longstanding legal problems.

Difficult issues related to land or other real estate might slowly but surely resolve themselves, and the result will be in your favor.

Employees can count on a promotion, which you will discuss this month. Closer to the end of October, or perhaps in November, you can expect positive results.

Money. Your financial position is sustainable in October; you are regularly receiving money, and significantly more of it. You can expect to receive the largest amounts on October 8, 9, 16, 17, 26, and 27.

Love and family. October is also a good month for reconnecting with old friends and partners.

Single people might be the object of someone's attention, but if you meet each other between October 1 and 18, then it is unlikely to last for long. This applies to both your personal life and work. The last ten days of October are a good time for a surprisingly pleasant encounter!

Spouses and unmarried couples might go on a trip, where they will enjoy themselves. If you travel between October 1 and 18, however, it is better to pick a destination you have visited before.

Mercury is the planet for contacts and travel, and it will be in retrograde from September 27 to October 18, which is when the stars do not recommend going anywhere or meeting anyone new. The best course of action is reconnecting with old friends!

Health. In October, you are feeling fantastic, and everyone is noticing how attractive you are.

Pisces

You can expect a month full of bothersome routine, where your focus is on discipline, following schedules, and shouldering your responsibilities.

Work. October is a time for major administrative tasks, as well as various tasks related to real estate. This is also a time for work responsibilities involving red tape and financial documentation.

Be careful! Mercury will be in retrograde from September 27 to October 18, and this is usually a time rife with errors and endless re-dos.

Any disagreements with friends or former mentors are slowly working themselves out, and there is hope on the horizon that soon, they will be entirely resolved. This is relevant for anyone with longstanding legal problems, as well as those who are going through tough times with like-minded people.

Generally speaking, your overall situation is improving, and all the problems you dealt with previously are fading away. Your time will come in 2022, so hold on! That's not much longer!

Money. Financially, it's smooth sailing – but that's all you can say. For all events this month, business associates or loved ones – a spouse, parents, or elder relatives – will put funds for any basic costs.

You might also receive credit or profits from successful real estate transactions.

Love and family. Many Pisces are fully immersed in their personal lives in October. Major repair projects, new furniture and appliances, or new décor are on the agenda. Those who hadn't been able to buy a home or new apartment before might do so suddenly in October, likely in the last ten days of the month.

Any difficult relationships with relatives that vexed you in the past are slowly improving, and in the very near future, you will be a welcome guest among your unpredictable relatives.

Health. In October, you are feeling less than energetic, so take care of yourself, avoid any fall colds and infections, and avoid exacerbating any old, chronic illness.

You might tend to gain weight, so it is worth following a balanced diet.

November

Aries

You can expect several serious professional tests in November, as well as personal conflicts. You can't fake your way out of this – there's no turning back, now!

Work. Entrepreneurs and managers of every level will have to defend their position all month. The issue is the financial state of your shared business, and conflicts with associates and adversaries. Most likely, you will have to accept that some of those you were counting on will not fulfill their promises. You will be disappointed by high-level members of society or an old friend.

One bright spot among the gloomy fall colors of this month will be your relationships with colleagues from another city or abroad. You will get off on the right foot, and that trend will continue through December.

Employees should be good listeners and resolve all work-related issues carefully and diplomatically all month, if you want to avoid any trouble. This is most relevant when it comes to your relationship with managers and their assistants.

The best time for any professional event is the last ten days of November, when delicate, challenging issues are likely to be magically resolved.

You will need compromise on all sides, and you will definitely find it. You will get what you wanted, and no one will be left disappointed by the result. Your gains may be more modest than you had planned earlier, but that is certainly better than nothing.

Money. Your financial situation is volatile in November. During the first twenty days of the month, many Aries, for various reasons, will lose large amounts of money, likely more than once.

The last ten days of the month are looking very bright, however. Any arguments over money will be over, and you can expect the largest amounts to come in on November 27-29.

Love and family. Your personal life is ambiguous. During the first twenty days of November, things will be challenging for couples, whether or not they are married. You might be irritated with each other, or have moral or financial disagreements. In some cases, the disagreements will be related to your children, and this especially applies to couples with children from different partners.

The stars recommend quietly getting through this period, since no one can prove anything to anyone else, anyway. This is not one of those times when truth is born out of an argument.

Trust in the last ten days of the month, when things will be much calmer, and your problems will not look so glaring, after all.

Things will start to work themselves out, so don't pressure your loved ones, and don't make any demands. Soon, everything will fall into place.

Health. Those who escaped professional and personal troubles this month might instead face health issues. Be attentive and take care of your body, avoid any fall colds or infections, and take care of any chronic illnesses, as well.

Taurus

This month, you will have to deal with two matters at once. First of all, why do others periodically declare war on you? And secondly – do you maybe bear any of the blame?

Work. Your success last month may have sparked a wave of annoyance among those around you. As a result, entrepreneurs and managers might once again face hostile adversaries, who will be unusually persistent in claiming something of yours.

But you are tough, and you weren't born yesterday. If things get really difficult, you might turn to a lawyer for help, or else count on a colleague from another city or abroad. In any case, you will find a resolution toward the end of November and December.

Employees will face stiff competition, though their position is strong, and the only thing you have to fear is fear itself.

What is the reason for this constant hostility? There are two possibilities – either your ideas are very new and original, or you somehow made a very serious mistake. But this really depends on the individual, and only you can solve what is actually happening.

Money. Financially, November is mostly neutral. Your income is modest, but your expenses are also minimal, so closer to the end of the month, you will find yourself in balance, again.

Love and family. Any Taureans who were spared trouble at work might face problems in their personal life. After several quiet months – September and October- your loved one might unexpectedly start airing various grievances, whether moral or more tangible and material in nature.

In a decisive moment, you are sure to say "no". In fairness, it is worth noting that you are likely to pay the price for that, but only what you think is right, no more, and no less. That is of course relevant for anyone who has been living in a war zone or planning on divorcing for some time.

Stable couples can work together to overcome any problems, by relying on love and wisdom.

Health. In November, you are not particularly energetic, and the troubles this month may leave you feeling unsettled.

Remember that doctors believe that nerves and emotional problems are behind all illnesses, and act accordingly. Keep a cool head as you solve your problems, which will benefit all areas of your stressful life.

Gemini

You have been moving ahead at a steady pace, but this month, you are unlikely to see much progress. The road ahead is winding, but you will manage everything!

Work. This month, those in the business world will once again face challenges. It might be that you have overcome a lot of obstacles in the past, but right now, you will have to take a step back and re-examine some annoying issues.

In some cases, an established relationship with colleagues in other cities or abroad may now need some attention and adjustments. Alternatively, you will have to go back to some legal issues, which have suddenly taken an unexpected twist.

On top of all that, you may run into unexpected audits, which will put a damper on some of your plans, but will not stall them entirely.

Employees should be careful with colleagues, as there is intrigue and other unhealthy dynamics brewing on your team.

Managers and entrepreneurs should be cautious when dealing with subordinates – someone might interfere with your plans, intentionally or not.

All relationships will become more difficult during the first twenty days of the month, and only get back on track during the last ten days of November. It seems that, once again, you are overcoming problems and finding your way, with minimal losses.

Money. Financially, November will be up and down. You will not end up penniless, but your expenses will be rather high. A lot of them may be related to your problems at work.

Love and family. Your personal life may occupy less of your time this month, compared to things at work. If you spend most of your time at home with your family or romantic partner, however, you can count on November bringing some secrets to light, which will complicate your relationship with those around you.

This goes for married and unmarried couples, so buckle up, especially if there are things you would prefer remained in the dark.

You might also experience problems with relatives, either your own or those of your partner. In that case, you can expect that your own secrets will be revealed, as well as those of your loved ones.

This will make relationships much more difficult, but things will stop short of outright catastrophe. Maybe both sides will think about things, talk it over, and manage to forgive and understand each other.

Health. The first twenty days of November will be challenging for your health. You might feel very weak, and see chronic conditions exacerbate.

Additionally, the stars strongly recommend being very careful while traveling, driving, or using electric appliances. There is a strong likelihood of injury or accident this month.

Cancer

This month, your motto is "I'll rest in my dreams". And it's true – you will put out one fire, only to see another one pop up elsewhere.

Work. The astrologist predicts painful issues this month, related to your personal life. But those who work constantly and view life through a professional lens might also face trouble at work.

During the first twenty days of the month, you might expect conflict with friends or former mentors. As it frequently does, the issue will revolve around money or other obligations you have to be reminded of.

You will reach a compromise during the last ten days of November, and you will have to give something up in order to get there, as well as turn to intermediaries.

Your relationship with colleagues from afar is going rather well, and it is very possible that this contact will allow you to start a new life and new job elsewhere.

Money. Financially, November is not a lucky month. You will be bleeding money, and, in some cases, that will be related to business, while in others, your personal life will be the culprit. Your largest expenses of all during this dark time may take place during the first twenty days of the month.

Love and family. For many Cancers, most of the action in November will take place at home. Parents might face problems involving their children, which will lead to emotional outbursts and major expenses.

In some cases, the underlying cause may be perennial "parents vs. children" issues. In other cases, you will have to spend money on your children's education, training, and development. Your spouse or another loved one may act as a peacekeeper and assistant in this area (even if you are now divorced).

This is a difficult month for couples, and you might find yourselves disappointed in each other. You might ask yourself time and again, "is this relationship really necessary? Is this what I dreamt of?" If this is not your first conflict, but a conflict that repeats itself over and over again, the answer is becoming very clear, now, and you are questioning the future of the relationship.

Health. In November, you are feeling energetic, but unsettled. The drama surrounding you this month may leave many Cancers feeling down by the end of November. If that sounds like you, remember that any unresolved problems will fade away, soon enough!

Leo

This month, it is worth temporarily putting your ambitions on hold. They aren't happening, right now. And that goes for both work and your personal life.

Work. You are facing one of the more difficult months of your work and career. Entrepreneurs and managers will once again find themselves facing conflict with associates when it comes to shared business. Any previous agreements will go out the window for the time being, and you are not the one expected to benefit from that.

If you recently did not get what you wanted, the stars warn that November is not the time to start trying to revise any agreements, even if you think that you have been slighted. November will bring nothing but conflict and emotional outbursts.

That advice is relevant for employees, too, as they are also going through a difficult time at work. You may see major changes underway at your organization, which will force you to think about leaving. It is not worth making any requests to management right now, or getting into any arguments with colleagues. Your best strategy is to take some time away and work on your home and family life, for now.

Money. November is not a promising month for your bank account, which is not surprising given the trends at work. Your expenses are not excessive, but you will not have any income, either. Keep an eye on your wallet and close to the end of November, you can expect a small amount of money to come in.

Love and family. Many Leos might be fully immersed in their personal life this month. You can expect problems in this area of your life, too, and they will beset both stable couples, and those whose relationships have been on the rocks for some time.

There is a strong possibility that your lives are about to go in different directions, and you will prefer it this way. This is the path the planets will take you on during the first twenty days of November.

Closer to the end of the month, however, children may serve as a bridge between warring spouses, and you should take advantage of this if you are wavering in your decision. If you have no doubts, then that advice is superfluous.

Alternatively, your loved one will face problems, which will worry the entire family. If this describes you, be patient, and help everyone, however you can.

Health. This month, you are feeling less than energetic, so take care of yourself and be vigilant.

Virgo

From time to time, problems from the past rear their ugly heads, unexpectedly. This is what you are facing in November. However, the chaos will not last long, so collect yourself and keep a cool head!

Work. During the first twenty days of the month, Virgos will face several obstacles. Do not try to rush things as you work to overcome them. Be careful and measured in everything you do.

In some cases, you will deal with endless disagreements with colleagues from other cities or abroad, or perhaps you see legal problems looming on the horizon, once again.

All of this will significantly complicate your position, and once again, you will be forced to come back to issues that gave you headaches all year long. This is temporary, however, and that will be clear during the last ten days of the month, when pressure from the stars will come down, somewhat. During this time, all of your problems from earlier in the month will be mitigated, and slowly, but surely, resolved.

Money. Financial issues will require heightened attention in November. Now is not the time to jump into any risky transactions or plan major purchases. Instead, you should keep an eye on your budget.

During the most difficult periods, you might receive help from loved ones, and that support will be both moral and material in nature.

Love and family. The first twenty days of November will also be hard on your personal life. You might face serious trouble with your relatives, perhaps due to major arguments, or problems among your close family members. Either way, you will have to get involved in their affairs, which will require time, energy, and resources.

During this time, your children, parents, and partner may all play an important role. One of them will act as an intermediary or assistant, and attempt to smooth things over.

Closer to the end of November, most of these painful, delicate issues will be resolved favorably.

Health. Throughout November, particularly the first twenty days of the month, the stars strongly urge that you be extra careful when driving and traveling. You face a high chance of accidents, injuries, or unfortunate incidents. It would be a good idea to avoid all travel, whether near or far, unless it is truly essential.

Libra

It will be hard for you to focus on just one thing in November – your home, loved ones, and routine tasks at work will all require your attention. In order to manage it all, draw up a plan of action and consult it regularly!

Work. During the first twenty days of November, financial issues may require special attention from you. Many Libras will have to examine their budget, because right now, some of your investment at work is excessive.

In many cases, there will be expenses related to expanding your business, buying real estate or land, or perhaps major construction projects. You might also have to shoulder obligations you took on earlier, related to friends, someone influential, or other circumstances in life.

Your relationship with colleagues in other cities and abroad is moving along with varying success, and some events in this part of your life might be clearly positive, but you will have to work for it – in short – just like anything else.

Money. November is a very difficult month for your finances, and for many Libras, it is downright negative. In some cases, your expenses may be related to business, while in others, your personal life, family obligations, and – most of all – children are the culprit.

Love and family. In your personal life, you will have to resolve matters related to your family and home. In some cases, you will have to deal with issues stemming from your children, and once again, this may not be free.

Be attentive and have a healthy dose of skepticism toward the events unfolding – once again, you may find yourself putting money into a black hole. After all, this situation has been going on for years, already, and every time, you pay up.

Nonetheless, this month, you have an excellent chance to put an end to this situation. Be honest and open, so everyone is on the same page – you will have the last word.

If the issue at hand is illness, school, or your children's development, then things are different. If that is the case, the expenses are justified, and who will pay them, if not you?

The stars recommend that you carefully analyze the situation – that will help to make the right decision, to benefit not only your children, but the entire family. Your spouse will help you in this endeavor, as will parents, and elder family members.

Couples again find their relationship under pressure from the stars. Here, you have to answer a question – is this a fling, or the love of your life? However, there is no point in trying to make a decision when feelings are mixed up with reason, so get through the stress of the first twenty days of November, and you will be able to make healthy decisions closer to the end of the month.

Health. This month, you are not particularly energetic, so take care of yourself and be vigilant; watch what you eat and drink. Remember that any experiments with your appearance during the first twenty days of the month may turn out to be a disaster.

Scorpio

You are celebrating your birth month in fighting mode. It seems that the struggle continues.

Work. This month, you will be up to your neck in work, as once again, problems loom on the horizon. After a peaceful October, entrepreneurs and managers will be surprised to discover that their adversaries are unwilling to fully comply with previous agreements, but you aren't willing to give in, either! You can expect several conflicts revolving around this during the first twenty days of November.

You might find yourself once again feuding over real estate or other major assets. You can expect a peaceful negotiation during the last ten days of November, or perhaps even in December. The astrologist sees victory on your side.

Employees should be attentive when dealing with managers, and avoid starting conflicts with colleagues. If someone slights you, be firm but diplomatic. Conflicts on your team might lead to the opposite of what you want. If you want to leave your job and company, however, do not heed this advice.

Money. The best time for your wallet in November is the last ten days of the month. You can also expect small sums of money to come in on

November 6, 7, 15, and 16.

Love and family. In your personal life, you can expect to face difficulties with roots in the past. Feuding spouses will again resume fighting over dividing up their shared real estate. Once again, the issue at hand is property, and you have been arguing over this all year. Earlier agreements have gone out the window for various reasons, and as a result, you will have to muster the will and defend your position with a vengeance.

Stable couples will have to struggle over property disputes, and your adversaries will be unscrupulous.

In all cases, this month might see you counting on help from relatives, whose influence throughout November might only be positive.

Health. In November, you are supported by Mars, the strongest source of energy, which means that you will definitely not fall by the wayside. The stars strongly suggest that you only use this excess energy for peaceful purposes and remember that the best fight is one that didn't happen.

Sagittarius

November will unexpectedly put you to the test, which will affect nearly every aspect of your life. Be careful and cautious, but don't give in!

Work. Sagittarians will face many problems at work this month. In some cases, this unpredictability will come from partners in other cities or abroad. In others, the law may stand in your way.

Somewhat unexpectedly, something you would have preferred stayed a secret may be revealed, which will have a negative impact on your work and reputation.

For most Sagittarians, your enemies and competition will become active and hold back at nothing when it comes to throwing a wrench in your plans. Entrepreneurs and managers should get ready for visits from auditing agencies, which might suddenly "pop in" during the first twenty days of November. Additionally, managers should be very attentive when dealing with subordinates, who may, due to either negligence or poor intentions, cast a shadow over your work.

Employees should be careful when dealing with colleagues, and not participate in any intrigue which might snowball and make November very difficult for you.

The most difficult time will be the first twenty days of November, when your problems may arise unexpectedly, and out of the blue. During this time, friends will attempt to lend a hand, but their influence will not be enough to resolve everything that you must face during this gloomy time of the year.

During the last ten days of November, things will feel calmer. You will be able to take control of the situation, and gradually move forward.

Money. Despite your problems at work, your bank account is feeling fine, for the most part. Venus will beautify the financial sector of your sky for most of the month, which means that you will not find yourself penniless. Money will come in regularly, and you can expect the largest sums on November 1, 8, 9, 17, 18, 27, and 28.

Your expenses are moderate, and most of them are both reasonable and predictable.

Love and family. For those who spend all their time at home, November is not an easy time, either. Your relationship with family members is growing difficult once again, and you might find out certain relatives' secrets, or they will find out yours. This will all lead to misunderstandings and conflicts, which will peak between November 11 and 20.

The stars advise you to be attentive and think before taking anyone's word. It is very possible that the information you receive is exaggerated, and someone is trying to deceive you. This is also relevant for couples, who may come under pressure from the heavens, as well.

Even if you don't end up in a tricky situation, remember that your problems will not last forever – by the end of November, the heavens above you will light up, which will create a favorable trend expected to continue into December.

Health. Anyone who was spared professional and personal drama this month may endure health issues, instead. During the first twenty days of the month you can expect sudden accidents and injuries.

Drivers should be very careful. It is best to avoid any travel, whether close to home or not, as it will lead to nothing but trouble. Anyone elderly or weakened should take extra steps to protect themselves – you are very likely to see any chronic health problems worsen this month.

Capricorn

This month, you might expect the unexpected – your emotions will prevail over logic, when you should strive for the opposite, which is the only way to exert any control over events in your personal and professional life.

Work. Just like last month, your career and work are your priorities this month. But right now, your goal is to strengthen your relationship with friends and influential members of society. That will not be an easy task, as in exchange for certain services, you may have to fulfill various demands. Most likely, that means money or other things of material value. But if you are ready for that kind of development, there is no way around it.

With the exception of this issue, work is still going well; your ties to colleagues from other cities or abroad are growing, and you may even go on a successful trip.

Many Capricorns are laying the groundwork for opening their own business in another city or abroad, and in 2022, that will become a reality.

Money. As far as finances are concerned, November might be bumpy. You might face major expenses all month long, and most of them will come during the first half of the month. In some cases, this may involve money paid to resolve work-related problems, and in others, it will be due to a difficult situation with your family, possibly your children's affairs.

Love and family. During the first twenty days of the month, you might have to deal with difficult situations, as well as delicate, sensitive matters.

Parents will have to deal with many problems involving their children, which will once again lead to emotional outbursts and unexpected expenses. You are aware of the problem, but this time, it may take a new, unpleasant turn for the entire family. During the second half of the month, things will improve, thanks to your good faith and effort. The problem may continue to cause you stress for some time, and the stars recommend that you carefully study the entire situation and its root cause. This is necessary, if you don't want things to repeat themselves later on.

For couples, November is also a challenging time. You can expect sudden conflicts from the very beginning of the month, and things will clear up a little later. You will see that there was, in fact, no major problem, and you will understand everything and forgive a lot. What's more, you are looking at the issue from a very close range. So, don't stick to hard and fast rules, take the first step, and you will be pleasantly surprised with your partner's reaction.

Health. This month, you are healthy, energetic, and attractive – and everyone fate sends your way is taking note.

Aquarius

The decisions you will have to make in November might have major, lasting consequences, so think things through carefully! The future is in your hands!

Work. This month, you will reach your peak at work, but not everything is going to turn out as you had hoped. You might have some disagreements with business partners, and once again, the problem revolves around real estate or other major assets. Right now, however, your position is stronger, and your adversaries will have to accept that.

That is why closer to the end of the month, things may improve, and you will achieve what you wanted. In any case, old friends or skilled attorneys will lend a helping hand this month.

Your development of ties with colleagues in other cities or abroad is November's silver lining. At the beginning of the month, you will be able to count on productive meetings, as well as good news from your associates located far away.

Employees might experience conflict with management during the first half of the month, though closer to the end of November, things will smooth over.

Money. Your financial outlook is looking stable, and you will have money coming in regularly, as well as more of it. You can expect the largest sums to come in on November 4, 5, 12, 13, 22, and 23.

Love and family. You will see a continuation of issues you have faced many times in the past, when it comes to your personal life. Once again, this involves disputes over real estate, which may haunt divorcing couples.

Despite the fact that these issues were all supposedly resolved long ago, you will have to come back to some of them, which will once again lead to conflict. But nothing is forever, so one way or another, these issues will be resolved for once and for all near the end of 2021.

During this time, stable couples might decisively handle unscrupulous adversaries. This time, the issue at hand is real estate or other major assets.

Health. In November, you are healthy, energetic, and have no risk of falling ill.

Pisces

November is a time for you to fight for what you believe in. Remember – victory is near! Soon, you will be beginning a new cycle in your life, and it will do away with everything that stressed you out before.

Work. During the first twenty days of November, entrepreneurs and managers will once again deal with problems from the past. In some cases, that may mean disagreements with colleagues from other cities or abroad, and in others, you will see old legal problems taking another turn.

In both cases, close to the end of the month, things will noticeably improve, and the problems will be resolved in December. In all cases, your old friends and some high-placed individuals will play an important, positive role this month. Their support will mitigate painful issues which have been bothering you for some time, and, in many cases, they will be resolved entirely.

Employees are likely to have negotiations about a new job near the need of the month, and entrepreneurs are likely to discuss a new business. In either case, things will continue on a positive track in December.

Money. In November, your finances may be up and down. Your income is not large, but your expenses are modest. Close to the end of the month, you will manage to strike a balance.

Love and family. Your personal life may take an unexpected and undesirable turn. You might have a difficult relationship with someone from your family, and this time, you can expect arguments, once again.

Your friends and someone close to you will attempt to mitigate the situation, and, thanks to their efforts, the conflict will gradually fade away, though that is only likely next month or in early 2022.

Health. This month, you are noticeably more energetic, but it's not worth testing your body's limits. Living a healthy lifestyle and being kind to yourself are still your best companions. Be attentive when traveling and driving! Accidents and unpleasant situations are highly likely, especially during the first twenty days of November.

December

Aries

December is the best time of the year for you, and in all cases, it is the most productive and dynamic month. You are taking the right steps right now, and making reasonable decisions, which will pay off in the near future.

Work. You will have a lot of work this month, and everything related to business and your career will be resolved favorably. Entrepreneurs and managers might complete a major project and implement necessary changes.

Employees will be noticed by management thanks to the obvious progress they are making at work.

Your relationship with colleagues from other cities or abroad is moving along nicely, overall, and you might have negotiations aimed at future cooperation. It seems everything is going extremely well, but remember the old proverb – "every rose has its thorn". That applies now, as well. One such thorn maybe your relationship with a friend or certain, high-level individuals, and the issue will revolve around money or other financial obligations, once again. This will be one of the most difficult issues of December, for you. The problem will be resolved in 2022, peacefully and favorably.

Money. When it comes to money, December is not bad at all. You will have money coming in regularly, and lots of it, and the large amounts you spend in late December will not reflect negatively on the overall situation this month. Everything is going great!

Love and family. Your personal life is less dynamic than work, right now. You are not facing any problems, here, and your loved ones will not be sidelined. Rather, they will help you in both words and deeds.

Your relatives will also have significant, positive influence in all professional and personal matters this month.

Your relationship with a friend will be a challenge this month, likely near the end of the month, when they will need financial, rather than moral support from you. Alternatively, you might have arguments over material demands.

Health. In December, you are feeling energetic, and are not likely to fall ill.

Taurus

In order to be on steady footing, you need to work tirelessly. That is how December will go for you.

Work. December is a month full of administrative tasks, in preparation for a quieter, more successful period, which will begin in January 2022.

Many Taureans will get their affairs and documents in order, while also tackling problems that have beset them all of 2021.

Once again, entrepreneurs will have to wage a battle over property claimed by overwhelming adversaries. Employees will again face rigidness from management.

Your links to colleagues from other cities or abroad will move forward nicely – this is one of the bright spots in December. In some cases, you may discuss cooperation, while in others, a move.

Those facing legal problems will be pleased with a favorable resolution, which will take place in late December, or perhaps in January 2022.

Money. When it comes to finances, December is rather difficult. Your expenses will be larger than your income, and in some cases, that stems from resolving professional quandaries, while in others, your home and family are the culprit.

Love and family. You will continue feel the aftershocks of a family feud in December, though this time, they are much quieter than before. In order to not ruin the holiday season, warring spouses will deal with their underlying issues in December. That is the right thing to do – why drag problems into 2022?

Stable couples might work together to resolve various everyday problems, such as decorating their home for the holidays.

Those planning on a trip will be able to carry out their ideas closer to the end of December, or perhaps early next year.

Health. In December, you are not particularly energetic, and that will be most noticeable during the New Moon and eclipse- December 4 and 5. During this period, conserve your energy and take care of yourself.

Gemini

The stars are urging you to help others, but don't forget about yourself. If you able to combine these two opposing trends, you are sure to win.

Work. Your business partners will exert powerful influence all month long. With their assistance, you will be able to resolve difficult relationships with colleagues in other cities or abroad, and reach the next level, professionally.

2021 has not been an easy year for you, but things are about to improve – you will feel calmer, and the road to success is opening right now.

December will not be easy, either, and you can expect various situations to become more difficult at both the beginning and end of the month. You may have to grapple with challenging relationships with colleagues from other cities or abroad, or possibly, you will have to deal with old legal problems, instead. In the end, though, everything will resolve in your favor, and closer to the end of the month, you will be able to celebrate your victory.

Money. Financially, you are also fighting an uphill battle. You will be spending constantly, and in some cases, that will stem from resolving issues at work, while in others, your home and family will be the source. During the worst periods, a business partner, spouse, parents, or other loved one may help you.

Love and family. Many Geminis will be busy with their personal life, and to a certain extent, follow the lead of a loved one. You will not have to wait long for a response. In return, you might receive support – either moral or financial – if you need it. If the issue concerns your relatives, which is very likely at the beginning or end of December, your partner might play a major role in resolving matters.

Many Geminis will have an encounter with a former partner who now lives in another city or abroad.

Those who are moving somewhere far away this month might have to resolve major domestic quandaries, such as how to set up a home somewhere new.

Health. You are not particularly energetic this month, and that is most noticeable as December comes to a close. During this time, remember to take care of yourself, take some time to relax, and get enough sleep.

Cancer

It's the last month of the year, and for you, that means it's a time of reckoning for old debts – whether moral or financial.

Work. You are about to begin one of the hardest periods of the year. Your biggest problem – a relationship with a friend or influential member of society – will not be resolved until the end of the month.

Again, this involves money, financial obligations, and it seems that not everything will be resolved until the very end.

This month, you will have to square away some old debts, and if someone owes you, you might be able to count on them paying you back. During thorny negotiations with your adversaries, you might receive help from an old friend or loved one. Moving forward, you can be assured of a brighter future, and, in many cases, that will take place somewhere far away from your home town.

You will also leave a painful past behind in December; this is necessary in order to open the doors to better things.

Money. Financially, December is very difficult. You will be spending constantly, perhaps due to work, or maybe your family.

Love and family. Your personal life is tumultuous and stressful, and the underlying reasons are different for everyone.

Parents will have to resolve problems involving their children and that will take up a large chunk of the family budget. If you find that task difficult, turn to a loved one for help; they will be able to shoulder some of the challenge themselves, even if you are fighting or divorcing.

For couples, December will bring challenges, as well. You will both have grievances about each other, which will seriously hamper your relationship, and in some cases, drive you to the brink of separation. If this is not the first feud in this love story, it might be the last.

Health. In December, you might not be feeling particularly confident or cheerful. In order to strike a balance, do not forget the power of taking a walk, even if the winter weather is not particularly inviting, and be sure to get enough sleep, too.

Leo

The end of the year will be a busy time, and you are sure to see a variety of events taking place. There is nothing you can do about that, it's just life!

Work. Your biggest problem in December will be your relationship with a business partner. You will have constant disagreements related to different visions of your business, and you may even part ways. This is most likely at the beginning and end of December.

This is an issue that has been going on for a while, and either improved or worsened, but now it is D-Day, and you will have to resolve this stagnant conflict, one way or another. What do you do? Only you can decide. You may decide to take out credit and buy out your adversaries in order to take the business yourself. Alternatively, you might receive a payment for your share, while your former business partner takes the rest.

You are unlikely to be capable of working together anymore, so each party might choose the option that is most favorable to themselves.

Things look much easier for employees – they can turn to management and strengthen their own fragile position.

Money. Your finances are looking unstable in December. You will have income, but you have massive expenses, and most of it is related to your home, family, children, or romantic relationships.

Love and family. Your family life is looking rather calm. Couples in a stable marriage will be busy with repairs, and they may decide to re-do their interiors. Many will resolve problems related to their children, and invest in their training, education, and development, which will take up a large chunk of the family budget.

Divorced and divorcing couples might have difficulty resolving residual issues involving property, and there is hope that this month, their saga will finally come to an end.

For many Leos, December is a time of celebrations, birthdays, and reconnecting with old friends and lovers. You might rekindle an old romance, and wonder about its future. You will spend the holidays themselves with children and your closest loved ones, however.

Health. This month, you will be healthy, energetic, and spared by any illness.

Virgo

The solar eclipse is driving many Virgos to pay extremely close attention to family matters and get on the right track. It's not worth letting these problems follow you into 2022!

Work. Virgos in the working world will once again have to devote time to the most painful topic of 2021. In some cases, that may be a difficult relationship with colleagues from other cities or abroad, and in others, longstanding legal problems.

This is all expected to come to a head again in early and late December, though this time, you are moving closer to a favorable resolution. Jupiter will be moving into a favorable section of your sky during the last days of the month. This means that you will meet new partners, who are both influential and reliable. All the problems that troubled you in 2021 will gradually fade away.

Money. Your financial situation will be very up and down this month. You will be spending constantly, which may be directly related to your family's and children's needs.

Those who work in construction or in a business somehow related to real estate or leisure will have more luck.

Love and family. Many of December's events will take place at home and with your family. You might have to work on home improvement, small repairs, décor, and the biggest holiday season of the year. In many cases, you will have to do the same for your older children.

Your relationship with relatives might once again become difficult, and this may involve either your family or your partner's. This is not a new situation, and it is not difficult to navigate. A feud cannot last forever, though, and that is the case now, as well. You can hope that this will be the last showdown, to be followed by peace.

Parents will be delighted with their children, who are showing strong progress, and this may even reconcile those whose relationship has long left much to be desired.

Couples are close to achieving their dreams. Soon, they will plan to get married or live together. If that does not happen in December, then it is highly likely that in 2022 you will have many opportunities to have someone by your side.

Health. In December, you are not particularly energetic, and the elderly or those weakened by chronic illness need to be especially vigilant.

Drivers and travelers should be careful – there is a high likelihood of accidents this month. The most challenging time is the first and the last ten days of the month.

Libra

All of December is a good time for you. You will take on any responsibilities and manage it skillfully. Your intelligence is on display!

Work. With regard to your professional life, December is a very successful time for you. You are likely to hold many meetings, and your best qualities – foresight, patience, and an ability to get out of sticky situations- will come in very handy.

You can expect to take multiple trips, both in your region and abroad. Be careful with the financial side of things during all of your negotiations this month – there is a real possibility of unexpected and unpleasant surprises. This may once again involve real estate, land, or other major assets. If you lay some trump cards on the table, sometimes that is enough to assert your position, if not entirely, at least in part.

Managers of all levels should still be careful with their subordinates – time has shown that someone needs to be replaced. In December, you will be in the talking, planning, and ideas phase, but closer to March 2022, everything you had been thinking about will suddenly begin to happen.

Employees are thinking about changing jobs, and that is clearly for the best. The astrologer suggests that it will be a promotion, likely within the same organization.

Money. Aggressive Mars is in the financial sector of your sky for most of the month, and that means that you will be spending more than you are bringing home. In many cases, your family life will be a very messy.

Love and family. Your personal life will continue to be rife with problems, which have caused you stress, all year long. Once again, this involves your children, and again, you will have to resolve something. Often, your children's problems will involve major expenses for you.

Divorcing couples might finally deal with difficult issues related to their home, while those in stable marriages will be busy getting their home or apartment in order.

Your relationship with relatives is improving, and one family member may help with both words and deeds.

Couples might jump out of the frying pan, into the fire all month long, and the stars strongly urge you to control your emotions and avoid any blowouts the night before any holidays. The likelihood of this is very high.

Health. This month, you are healthy, energetic, charming, and ready to move mountains.

Scorpio

This month, you might be a worker, in the strictest sense of the word. You will work hard, and as a result, you can call yourself one of those chosen by Fortune. What more can you want?

Work. There is a good chance that you will achieve some of your most important goals for 2021 in December. Both entrepreneurs and managers will be able to resolve many difficult quandaries related to land or real estate in early or late December, after some delicate negotiations.

Your relationship with colleagues from far away is moving along nicely, and you can expect productive negotiations, which is most relevant for those who are planning to work in another city or abroad.

Any travel planned for December will be very successful. Closer to the end of the year, you will see some good results, and that trend will continue into 2022.

Money. Your financial outlook in December is excellent. You will regularly receive money, and significantly more of it, as well. You might even say that when it comes to material things, December is one of the best months of the year for you.

You can expect the largest sums on December 4, 5, 12, 13, 22, 23, and 31.

Love and family. Your personal life is sure to see the continuation of processes that began earlier. This includes disputes over some real estate, possibly between divorcing couples.

You will also have to resolve an issue over large assets with unscrupulous individuals. Thanks to your persistence, you are sure to resolve this matter, in your favor, of course!

Relatives may play a major role in the developments underway this month. They are on a winning streak, and happy to share their success with you – both moral and material support.

Children will bring joy – you are starting to see a wonderful period when it comes to them. Many families are growing, adding either children or grandchildren.

Health. This month, you are healthy, energetic, and the stars suggest you use that energy for peaceful purposes, only!

Sagittarius

This year has caused you a lot of anxiety, as well as changes in every area of your life. You are better at handling this than most, after all, don't you work best under pressure?

Work. The eclipse, which is now moving into your sign, is forcing you to be active and decisive. Thanks to that, you will quickly tackle your problems from last month, and impose your rules of the game.

Difficult relationships with colleagues from other cities or abroad will gradually improve. Even if you still have some disagreements, which are very likely in early or late December, that will not reflect on the favorable way things are going.

Challenging relationships with colleagues and subordinates will also be resolved favorably. Managers might have to give their team members raises or bonuses, in order to keep everyone happy and cooperative. Fortunately, you will find the money for it.

Those looking to launch their business in another city or abroad after the anxiety of 2021 will be close to making their dreams a reality.

Money. This month, your wallet is looking very healthy, and you will regularly receive money, and significantly more of it, too. You can expect to receive the largest sums on December 6, 7, 14-16, and 24-26. But there are no gifts here – you have earned everything honestly, through hard work. Those who are young and just starting out might receive help from their parents.

Love and family. Your personal life is much calmer, now. This month, you are at the real center of your family. You may find friends, relatives, and children around you, and you will find a kind word and tangible, financial support for all of them.

You will also see your relatives, and you might resolve previous issues, at least in part, if not entirely.

Anyone planning to move this month might look for a place to live. That may be a new home, a new apartment, or a modest home in the country. In other cases, this will happen in another city or abroad.

This month will be kind to couples – their relationship with parents and relatives is now much better, and many of them are making plans involving marriage or living together.

Health. This month, you are healthy, energetic, and very attractive. Everyone fate places in your path is noticing, too. During the first and last ten days of December, however, you be careful when traveling and driving. There is a high chance of accidents, injuries, and unfortunate incidents during this period.

Capricorn

The last month, you have been working on a difficult task in unfamiliar waters. The past and future are strangely intertwined, and you need to say goodbye to the former and accept the latter.

Work. December is a time of transition from a period of high anxiety in the past, to an unusual and very positive future.

Your problems from the past include a challenging relationship with an adversary. Once again, you will have to deal with grievances, which are most likely financial in nature. You might also face audits or even legal problems.

Along with that, entrepreneurs will once again have an idea for expanding their business, but this time, in another city or abroad. In order to reach that goal, you must take advantage of all of your contacts. If you do, you won't have to wait long to see results. Though you are only in the negotiation phase, these are the first steps in the right direction, and there is no doubt that 2022 is the year you will make things happen.

Changes at work will also affect employees, most all when it comes to changes in the organizational structure of your workplace, which may spark various types of intrigue and competition.

Money. Your financial situation is contradictory. On one hand, you will not find yourself without any money at all. On the other, though, your expenses will be very high in December. This may be related to your issues at work, as well as your family and personal relationships.

Love and family. Your personal life may once again be full of problems from previous months. You will do everything in order to help your children, and a lot of your efforts will pay off. But they will need money once again, and you will have to give it to them. There is hope that in the near future, this issue will be entirely behind you, and next year, it shouldn't stress you, anymore.

Many Capricorns are on the brink of major changes – your plans may be related to a move, which might play out in 2022. You may move in town, to a home in the country, or possibly abroad.

Couples might find themselves arguing frequently and periodically wondering if they should break things off. But if your love is still alive, it will have the last say, over your rigidity, stinginess, pride, and ambitions. That is the way it should be, anyway!

Health. This month, you are not very energetic, and that will be most notable during the new moon and eclipse – December 4 and 5. Be careful and take it easy for a few days. The work will still be there tomorrow. During the first half of December, that is particularly relevant advice.

Aquarius

The future flows out of the present, and the present began in the past. This is a surprising month, when all temporal elements threaten to join forces.

Work. The most important thing this month is to have a benevolent relationship with those around you. That is relevant for all Aquarians, without exceptions, regardless of their field.

Your problems with management or the powers that be began in November, and during the first half of December, they may continue. But this time, things have improved, somewhat. Old friends or an influential mentor might bring an olive branch, this time. "Contacts are everything" – this is always relevant, but this time, it is especially important to keep in mind. If you keep this in mind, you will be able to significantly improve your image as well as your position at work.

Gradually, you will resolve any issues related to land and real estate which have caused entrepreneurs anxiety for some time, now. Negotiations on this topic will continue all month, and conclude in February 2022. This is not a quick endeavor, but the results will be very positive.

Your earlier problems will be resolved, and slowly but surely, you are laying the groundwork for a snapshot of your professional future. More likely than not, it is related to strengthening your position at work, and improving your material standing, through hard work and continuing along your chosen path.

Money. Your financial outlook in December is unstable. You will spend constantly, and most of it will be related to resolving problems at work. You might expect to receive some sums of money on December 1-3, 10-11, 20-21, and 30.

Love and family. Your personal life is now worsening, most likely involving a divorcing couple who have been disputing shared property, probably real estate, for some time, now.

You can expect more complaints, at the beginning and end of the month, but the situation will improve during the last days of December, or perhaps in January, when you are able to celebrate your victory.

Stable couples are at a turning point in their relationship with treacherous adversaries. Here, you can also expect problems related to real estate.

Unmarried couples might see very little of each other, but there is no reason for hurt feelings. Be patient, and your relationship will have less trouble. That goes for both you and your partner.

Health. In December, you are feeling energized, though close to the end of the month, you might feel fatigued after a difficult year. The stars recommend that you have a quiet holiday break with time to yourself and with your loved ones.

Pisces

The solar eclipse will take place in the highest part of your sky, and that means that December will be one of the busiest times of 2021 for you, and one of the luckiest, too.

Work. Change awaits most Pisces at work. You might get offers for a new job or start a new business, which will revive your professional life and financial outlook. Agreements reached in December might have lasting consequences, so there is good reason to pay close attention – your future is at stake!

At the same time, your previous problems are still relevant, most of all, your difficult relationship with colleagues in other cities or abroad, as well as legal matters. In either case, you can expect things to be difficult at the beginning and end of the month, but there is reason to hope that this will be the last time.

Your friends or high-level mentors might play a major role in optimizing these negative events, and their influence in all areas this month will be nothing but positive.

Money. December is a good month for you, financially. You are receiving regular income, and can expect the largest sums to come in on December 4, 5, 12, 13, 22, 23, and 31.

Love and family. In most cases, your personal life might be less exciting than work. Those who spend most of their time focused on family or romantic interests will also see longstanding problems involving close relatives resolved this month.

You might see hostilities spike again in early or late December, though this time, an old friend may serve as an intermediary. You will reach a compromise with family members, and in 2022, the situation will improve to an acceptable standard.

Issues related to your home will be resolved favorably, and many families will celebrate the holidays in a fully refurbished home or apartment.

Health. This month, you are feeling fairly energetic and are at no risk of falling ill. During the first or last ten days of the month, be careful when traveling or driving There is a very high likelihood of accidents and injuries during these periods.

A guide to Zodiac compatibility

Often, when we meet a person, we get a feeling that they are good and we take an instant liking to them. Another person, however, gives us immediate feelings of distrust, fear and hostility. Is there an astrological reason why people say that 'the first impression is the most accurate'? How can we detect those who will bring us nothing but trouble and unhappiness?

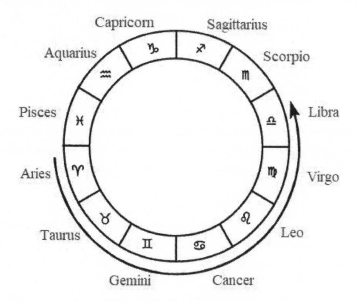

Without going too deeply into astrological subtleties unfamiliar to some readers, it is possible to determine the traits according to which friendship, love or business relationships will develop.

Let's begin with problematic relationships - our most difficult are with our **8th sign**. For example, for Aries the 8th sign is Scorpio, for Taurus it is Sagittarius and so on. Finding your 8th sign is easy; assume your own sign to be first (see above Figure) and then move eight signs counter clockwise around the Zodiac circle. This is also how the other signs (fourth, ninth and so on) that we mention are to be found.

Ancient astrologers variously referred to the 8th sign as the symbol of death, of destruction, of fated love or unfathomable attraction. In astrological terms, this pair is called 'master and slave' or 'boa constrictor and rabbit', with the role of 'master' or 'boa constrictor' being played by our 8th sign.

This relationship is especially difficult for politicians and business people.

We can take the example of a recent political confrontation in the USA. Hilary Clinton is a Scorpio while Donald Trump is a Gemini - her 8th sign. Even though many were certain that Clinton would be elected President, she lost.

To take another example, Hitler was a Taurus and his opponents – Stalin and Churchill - were both of his 8th sign, Sagittarius. The result of their confrontation is well known. Interestingly, the Russian Marshals who dealt crushing military blows to Hitler and so helped end the Third Reich - Konstantin Rokossovsky and Georgy Zhukov - were also Sagittarian, Hitler's 8th sign.

In another historical illustration, Lenin was also a Taurus. Stalin was of Lenin's 8th sign and was ultimately responsible for the downfall and possibly death of his one-time comrade-in-arms.

Business ties with those of our 8th sign are hazardous as they ultimately lead to stress and loss; both financial and moral. So, do not tangle with your 8th sign and never fight with it - your chances of winning are remote!

Such relationships are very interesting in terms of love and romance, however. We are magnetically attracted to our 8th sign and even though it may be very intense physically, it is very difficult for family life;

'Feeling bad when together, feeling worse when apart'.

As an example, let us take the famous lovers - George Sand who was Cancer and Alfred de Musset who was Sagittarius. Cancer is the 8th sign for Sagittarius, and the story of their crazy two-year love affair was the subject of much attention throughout France. Critics and writers were divided into 'Mussulist' and 'Sandist' camps; they debated fiercely about who was to blame for the sad ending to their love story - him or her. It's hard to imagine the energy needed to captivate the public for so long, but that energy was destructive for the couple. Passion raged in their hearts, but neither of them was able to comprehend their situation.

Georges Sand wrote to Musset, "*I ⸱on't love you anymore, an⸱ I will always a⸱ore you. I ⸱on't want you anymore, an⸱ I can't ⸱o without you. It seems that nothing but a heavenly lightning strike can heal me by ⸱estroying me. Goo⸱-bye! Stay or go, but ⸱on't say that I am not suffering. This is the only thing that can make me suffer even more, my love, my life, my bloo⸱! Go away, but kill me, leaving.*" Musset replied only in brief, but its power surpassed Sand's tirade, "*When you embrace⸱ me, I felt something that is still bothering me, making it impossible for me to approach another woman.*" These two people loved each other passionately and for two years lived together in a powder keg of passion, hatred and treachery.

When someone enters into a romantic liaison with their 8th sign, there will be no peace; indeed, these relationships are very attractive to those who enjoy the edgy, the borderline and, in the Dostoevsky style, the melodramatic. The first to lose interest in the relationship is, as a rule, the 8th sign.

If, by turn of fate, our child is born under our 8th sign, they will be very different from us and, in some ways, not live up to our expectations. It may be best to let them choose their own path.

In business and political relationships, the combination with our **12th sign** is also a complicated one.

We can take two political examples. Angela Merkel is a Cancer while Donald Trump is a Gemini - her 12th sign. This is why their relations are strained and complicated and we can even perhaps assume that the American president will achieve his political goals at her expense. Boris Yeltsin (Aquarius) was the 12th sign to Mikhail Gorbachev (Pisces) and it was Yeltsin who managed to dethrone the champion of Perestroika.

Even ancient astrologers noticed that our relationships with our 12th signs can never develop evenly; it is one of the most curious and problematic combinations. They are our hidden enemies and they seem to be digging a hole for us; they ingratiate themselves with us, discover our innermost secrets. As a result, we become bewildered and make mistakes when we deal with them. Among the Roman emperors murdered by members of their entourage, there was an interesting pattern - all the murderers were the 12th sign of the murdered.

We can also see this pernicious effect in Russian history: the German princess Alexandra (Gemini) married the last Russian Tsar Nicholas II (Taurus) - he was her 12th sign and brought her a tragic death. The wicked genius Grigory Rasputin (Cancer) made friends with Tsarina Alexandra, who was his 12th sign, and was murdered as a result of their odd friendship. The weakness of Nicholas II was exposed, and his authority reduced after the death of the economic and social reformer Pyotr Stolypin, who was his 12th sign. Thus, we see a chain of people whose downfall was brought about by their 12th sign.

So, it makes sense to be cautious of your 12th sign, especially if you have business ties. Usually, these people know much more about us than we want them to and they will often reveal our secrets for personal gain if it suits them. However, the outset of these relationships is, as a rule, quite normal - sometimes the two people will be friends, but sooner or later one will betray the other one or divulge a secret; inadvertently or not.

In terms of romantic relationships, our 12th sign is gentle, they take care of us and are tender towards us. They know our weaknesses well but accept them with understanding. It is they who guide us, although sometimes almost imperceptibly. Sexual attraction is usually strong.

For example, Meghan Markle is a Leo, the 12th sign for Prince Harry, who is a Virgo. Despite Queen Elizabeth II being lukewarm about the match, Harry's love was so strong that they did marry.

If a child is our 12th sign, it later becomes clear that they know all our secrets, even those that they are not supposed to know. It is very difficult to control them as they do everything in their own way.

Relations with our 7th **sign** are also interesting. They are like our opposite; they have something to learn from us while we, in turn, have something to learn from them. This combination, in business and personal relationships, can be very positive and stimulating provided that both partners are quite intelligent and have high moral standards but if not, constant misunderstandings and challenges follow. Marriage or co-operation with the 7th sign can only exist as the union of two fully-fledged individuals and in this case love, significant business achievements and social success are possible.

However, the combination can be not only interesting, but also quite complicated.

An example is Angelina Jolie, a Gemini, and Brad Pitt, a Sagittarius. This is a typical bond with a 7th sign - it's lively and interesting, but rather stressful. Although such a couple may quarrel and even part from time to time, never do they lose interest in each other.

This may be why this combination is more stable in middle-age when there is an understanding of the true nature of marriage and partnership. In global, political terms, this suggests a state of eternal tension - a cold war - for example between Yeltsin (Aquarius) and Bill Clinton (Leo).

Relations with our 9th **sign** are very good; they are our teacher and advisor - one who reveals things we are unaware of and our relationships with them very often involve travel or re-location. The combination can lead to spiritual growth and can be beneficial in terms of business.

Although, for example, Trump and Putin are political opponents, they can come to an understanding and even feel a certain sympathy for each other because Putin is a Libra while Trump is a Gemini, his 9th sign.

This union is also quite harmonious for conjugal and romantic relationships.

We treat our **3rd sign** somewhat condescendingly. They are like our younger siblings; we teach them and expect them to listen attentively. Our younger brothers and sisters are more often than not born under this sign. In terms of personal and sexual relationships, the union is not very inspiring and can end quickly, although this is not always the case. In terms of business, it is fairly average as it often connects partners from different cities or countries.

We treat our **5th sign** as a child and we must take care of them accordingly. The combination is not very good for business, however, since our 5th sign triumphs over us in terms of connections and finances, and thereby gives us very little in return save for love or sympathy. However, they are very good for family and romantic relationships, especially if the 5th sign is female. If a child is born as a 5th sign to their parents, their relationship will be a mutually smooth, loving and understanding one that lasts a lifetime.

Our **10th sign** is a born leader. Depending on the spiritual level of those involved, both pleasant and tense relations are possible; the relationship is often mutually beneficial in the good times but mutually disruptive in the bad times. In family relations, our 10th sign always tries to lead and will do so according to their intelligence and upbringing.

Our **4th sign** protects our home and can act as a sponsor to strengthen our financial or moral positions. Their advice should be heeded in all cases as it can be very effective, albeit very unobtrusive. If a woman takes this role, the relationship can be long and romantic, since all the spouse's wishes are usually met one way or another. Sometimes, such couples achieve great social success; for instance, Hilary Clinton, a Scorpio is the 4th sign to Bill Clinton, a Leo. On the other hand, if the husband is the 4th sign for his wife, he tends to be henpecked. There is often a strong sexual attraction. Our 4th sign can improve our living conditions and care for us in a parental way. If a child is our 4th sign, they are close to us and support us affectionately.

Relations with our **11th sign** are often either friendly or patronizing; we treat them reverently, while they treat us with friendly condescension. Sometimes, these relationships develop in an 'older brother' or 'high-ranking friend' sense; indeed, older brothers and sisters are often our 11th sign. In terms of personal and sexual relationships, our 11th sign is always inclined to enslave us. This tendency is most clearly manifested in such alliances as Capricorn and Pisces or Leo and Libra. A child who is the 11th sign to their parents will achieve greater success than their parents, but this will only make the parents proud.

Our **2nd sign** should bring us financial or other benefits; we receive a lot from them in both our business and our family life. In married couples, the 2nd sign usually looks after the financial situation for the benefit of the family. Sexual attraction is strong.

Our **6th sign** is our 'slave'; we always benefit from working with them and it's very difficult for them to escape our influence. In the event of hostility, especially if they have provoked the conflict, they receive a powerful retaliatory strike. In personal relations, we can almost destroy them by making them dance to our tune. For example, if a husband doesn't allow his wife to work or there are other adverse family circumstances, she gradually becomes lost as an individual despite being surrounded by care. This is the best-case scenario; worse outcomes are possible. Our 6th sign has a strong sexual attraction to us because we are the fatal 8th sign for them; we cool down quickly, however, and often make all kinds of demands. If the relationship with our 6th sign is a long one, there is a danger that routine, boredom and stagnation will ultimately destroy the relationship. A child born under our 6th sign needs particularly careful handling as they can feel fear or embarrassment when communicating with us. Their health often needs increased attention and we should also remember that they are very different from us emotionally.

Finally, we turn to relations with **our own sign**. Scorpio with Scorpio and Cancer with Cancer get along well, but in most other cases, however, our own sign is of little interest to us as it has a similar energy.

Sometimes, this relationship can develop as a rivalry, either in business or in love.

There is another interesting detail - we are often attracted to one particular sign. For example, a man's wife and mistress often have the same sign. If there is confrontation between the two, the stronger character displaces the weaker one. As an example, Prince Charles is a Scorpio, while both Princess Diana and Camilla Parker Bowles were born under the sign of Cancer. Camilla was the more assertive and became dominant.

Of course, in order to draw any definitive conclusions, we need an individually prepared horoscope, but the above always, one way or another, manifests itself.

Love description of Zodiac Signs

We know that human sexual behavior has been studied at length. Entire libraries have been written about it, with the aim of helping us understand ourselves and our partners. But is that even possible? It may not be; no matter how smart we are, when it comes to love and sex, there is always an infinite amount to learn. But we have to strive for perfection, and astrology, with its millennia of research, twelve astrological types, and twelve zodiac signs, may hold the key. Below, you will find a brief and accurate description of each zodiac sign's characteristics in love, for both men and women.

Men

ARIES

Aries men are not particularly deep or wise, but they make up for it in sincerity and loyalty. They are active, even aggressive lovers, but a hopeless romantic may be lurking just below the surface. Aries are often monogamous and chivalrous men, for whom there is only one woman (of course, in her absence, they can sleep around with no remorse). If the object of your affection is an Aries, be sure to give him a lot of sex, and remember that for an Aries, when it comes to sex, anything goes. Aries cannot stand women who are negative or disheveled. They need someone energetic, lively, and to feel exciting feelings of romance.

The best partner for an Aries is Cancer, Sagittarius, or Leo. Aquarius can also be a good match, but the relationship will be rather friendly in nature. Partnering with a Scorpio or Taurus will be difficult, but they can be stimulating lovers for an Aries. Virgos are good business contacts, but a poor match as lovers or spouses.

TAURUS

A typical Taurean man is warm, friendly, gentle, and passionate, even if he doesn't always show it. He is utterly captivated by the beauty of the female body, and can find inspiration in any woman. A Taurus has such excess physical and sexual prowess, that to him, sex is a way to relax and calm down. He is the most passionate and emotional lover of the Zodiac, but he expects his partner to take the initiative, and if she doesn't, he will easily find someone else. Taureans rarely divorce, and are true to the end – if not sexually, at least spiritually. They are secretive, keep their cards close, and may have secret lovers. If a Taurus does not feel a deep emotional connection with someone, he won't be shy to ask her friends for their number. He prefers a voluptuous figure over an athletic or skinny woman.

The best partners for a Taurus are Cancer, Virgo, Pisces, or Scorpio. Sagittarius can show a Taurus real delights in both body and spirit, but they are unlikely to make it down the aisle. They can have an interesting relationship with an Aquarius – these signs are very different, but sometimes can spend their lives together. They might initially feel attracted to an Aries, before rejecting her.

GEMINI

The typical Gemini man is easygoing and polite. He is calm, collected, and analytical. For a Gemini, passion is closely linked to intellect, to the point that they will try to find an explanation for their actions before carrying them out. But passion cannot be explained, which scares a Gemini, and they begin jumping from one extreme to the other. This is why you will find more bigamists among Geminis than any other sign of the Zodiac. Sometimes, Gemini men even have two families, or divorce and marry several times throughout the course of their lives. This may be because they simply can't let new and interesting experiences pass them by. A Gemini's wife or lover needs to be smart, quick, and always looking ahead. If she isn't, he will find a new object for his affection.

Aquarians, Libras, and Aries make good partners for a Gemini. A Sagittarius can be fascinating for him, but they will not marry before he reaches middle age, as both partners will be fickle while they are younger. A Gemini and Scorpio are likely to be a difficult match, and the Gemini will try to wriggle out of the Scorpio's tight embrace. A Taurus will be an exciting sex partner, but their partnership won't be for long, and the Taurus is often at fault.

CANCER

Cancers tend to be deep, emotional individuals, who are both sensitive and highly sexual. Their charm is almost mystical, and they know how to use it. Cancers may be the most promiscuous sign of the Zodiac, and open to absolutely anything in bed. Younger Cancers look for women who are more mature, as they are skilled lovers. As they age, they look for someone young enough to be their own daughter, and delight in taking on the role of a teacher. Cancers are devoted to building a family and an inviting home, but once they achieve that goal, they are likely to have a wandering eye. They will not seek moral justification, as they sincerely believe it is simply something everyone does. Their charm works in such a way that women are deeply convinced they are the most important love in a Cancer's life, and that circumstances are the only thing preventing them from being together. Remember that a Cancer man is a master manipulator, and will not be yours unless he is sure you have throngs of admirers. He loves feminine curves, and is turned on by exquisite fragrances. Cancers don't end things with old lovers, and often go back for a visit after a breakup. Another type of Cancer is rarer – a faithful friend, and up for anything in order to provide for his wife and children. He is patriotic and a responsible worker.

Scorpios, Pisces, and other Cancers are a good match. A Taurus can make for a lasting relationship, as both signs place great value on family and are able to get along with one another. A Sagittarius will result in fights and blowouts from the very beginning, followed by conflicts and breakups. The Sagittarius will suffer the most. Marriage to an Aries isn't off the table, but it won't last very long.

LEO

A typical Leo is handsome, proud, and vain, with a need to be the center of attention at all times. They often pretend to be virtuous, until they are able to actually master it. They crave flattery, and prefer women who comply and cater to them. Leos demand unconditional obedience, and constant approval. When a Leo is in love, he is fairly sexual, and capable of being devoted and faithful. Cheap love affairs are not his thing, and Leos are highly aware of how expensive it is to divorce. They make excellent fathers. A Leo's partner needs to look polished and well-dressed, and he will not tolerate either frumpiness or nerds.

Aries, Sagittarius, and Gemini make for good matches. Leos are often very beguiling to Libras; this is the most infamous astrological "master-slave" pairing. Leos are also inexplicably drawn to Pisces – this is the only sign capable of taming them. A Leo and Virgo will face a host of problems sooner or later, and they might be material in nature. The Virgo will attempt to conquer him, and if she does, a breakup is inevitable.

VIRGO

Virgo is a highly intellectual sign, who likes to take a step back and spend his time studying the big picture. But love inherently does not lend itself to analysis, and this can leave Virgos feeling perplexed. While Virgo is taking his time, studying the object of his affection, someone else will swoop in and take her away, leaving him bitterly disappointed. Perhaps for that reason, Virgos tend to marry late, but once they are married, they remain true, and hardly ever initiate divorce. In bed, they are modest and reserved, as they see sex as some sort of quirk of nature, designed solely for procreation. Most Virgos have a gifted sense of taste, hearing, and smell. They cannot tolerate pungent odors and can be squeamish; they believe their partners should always take pains to be very clean. Virgos usually hate over-the-top expressions of love, and are immune to sex as a mean s of control. Many Virgos are stingy and more appropriate as husbands than lovers. Male Virgos tend to be monogamous, though if they are unhappy or disappointed with their partner, they may begin to look for comfort elsewhere and often give in to drunkenness.

Taurus, Capricorn, and Scorpio make the best partners for a Virgo. They may feel inexplicable attraction for Aquarians. They will form friendships with Aries, but rarely will this couple make it down the aisle. With Leos, be careful – this sign is best as a lover, not a spouse.

LIBRA

Libra is a very complex, wishy-washy sign. They are constantly seeking perfection, which often leaves them in discord with the reality around them. Libra men are elegant and refined, and expect no less from their partner. Many Libras treat their partners like a beautiful work of art, and have trouble holding onto the object of their affection. They view love itself as a very abstract concept, and can get tired of the physical aspect of their relationship. They are much more drawn to intrigue and the chase- dreams, candlelit evenings, and other symbols of romance. A high percentage of Libra men are gay, and they view sex with other men as the more elite option. Even when Libras are unhappy in their marriages, they never divorce willingly. Their wives might leave them, however, or they might be taken away by a more decisive partner.

Aquarius and Gemini make the best matches for Libras. Libra can also easily control an independent Sagittarius, and can easily fall under the influence of a powerful and determined Leo, before putting all his strength and effort into breaking free. Relationships with Scorpios are difficult; they may become lovers, but will rarely marry.

SCORPIO

Though it is common to perceive Scorpios as incredibly sexual, they are, in fact, very unassuming, and never brag about their exploits. They will, however, be faithful and devoted to the right woman. The Scorpio man is taciturn, and you can't expect any tender words from him, but he will defend those he loves to the very end. Despite his outward control, Scorpio is very emotional; he needs and craves love, and is willing to fight for it. Scorpios are incredible lovers, and rather than leaving them tired, sex leaves them feeling energized. They are always sexy, even if they aren't particularly handsome. They are unconcerned with the ceremony of wooing you, and more focused on the act of love itself.

Expressive Cancers and gentle, amenable Pisces make the best partners. A Scorpio might also fall under the spell of a Virgo, who is adept at taking the lead. Sparks might fly between two Scorpios, or with a Taurus, who is perfect for a Scorpio in bed. Relationships with Libras, Sagittarians, and Aries are difficult.

SAGITTARIUS

Sagittarian men are lucky, curious, and gregarious. Younger Sagittarians are romantic, passionate, and burning with desire to experience every type of love. Sagittarius is a very idealistic sign, and in that search for perfection, they tend to flit from one partner to another, eventually forgetting what they were even looking for in the first place. A negative Sagittarius might have two or three relationships going on at once, assigning each partner a different day of the week. On the other hand, a positive Sagittarius will channel his powerful sexual energy into creativity, and take his career to new heights. Generally speaking, after multiple relationships and divorces, the Sagittarian man will conclude that his ideal marriage is one where his partner is willing to look the other way.

Aries and Leo make the best matches for a Sagittarius. He might fall under the spell of a Cancer, but would not be happy being married to her. Gemini can be very intriguing, but will only make for a happy marriage after middle age, when both partners are older and wiser. Younger Sagittarians often marry Aquarian women, but things quickly fall apart. Scorpios can make for an interesting relationship, but if the Sagittarius fails to comply, divorce is inevitable.

CAPRICORN

Practical, reserved Capricorn is one of the least sexual signs of the Zodiac. He views sex as an idle way to pass the time, and something he can live without, until he wants to start a family. He tends to marry late, and almost never divorces. Young Capricorns are prone to suppressing their sexual desires, and only discover them later in life, when they have already achieved everything a real man needs – a career and money. We'll be frank – Capricorn is not the best lover, but he can compensate by being caring, attentive, and showering you with valuable gifts. Ever cautious, Capricorn loves to schedule his sexual relationships, and this is something partners will just have to accept. Women should understand that Capricorn needs some help relaxing – perhaps with alcohol. They prefer inconspicuous, unassuming women, and run away from a fashion plate.

The best partners for a Capricorn are Virgo, Taurus, or Scorpio. Cancers might catch his attention, and if they marry, it is likely to be for life. Capricorn is able to easily dominate Pisces, and Pisces-Capricorn is a well-known "slave and master" combination. Relationships with Leos tend to be erratic, and they are unlikely to wed. Aries might make for a cozy family at first, but things will cool off quickly, and often, the marriage only lasts as long as Capricorn is unwilling to make a change in his life.

AQUARIUS

Aquarian men are mercurial, and often come off as peculiar, unusual, or aloof, and detached. Aquarians are turned on by anything novel or strange, and they are constantly looking for new and interesting people. They are stimulated by having a variety of sexual partners, but they consider this to simply be normal life, rather than sexually immoral. Aquarians are unique – they are more abstract than realistic, and can be cold and incomprehensible, even in close relationships. Once an Aquarius gets married, he will try to remain within the realm of decency, but often fails. An Aquarian's partners need uncommon patience, as nothing they do can restrain him. Occasionally, one might encounter another kind of Aquarius – a responsible, hard worker, and exemplary family man.

The best matches for an Aquarius are female fellow Aquarians, Libras, and Sagittarians. When Aquarius seeks out yet another affair, he is not choosy, and will be happy with anyone.

PISCES

Pisces is the most eccentric sign of the Zodiac. This is reflected in his romantic tendencies and sex life. Pisces men become very dependent on those with whom they have a close relationship. Paradoxically, they are simultaneously crafty and childlike when it comes to playing games, and they are easily deceived. As a double bodied sign, Pisces rarely marry just once, as they are very sexual, easily fall in love, and are constantly seeking their ideal. Pisces are very warm people, who love to take care of others and are inclined toward "slave-master" relationships, in which they are the submissive partner. But after catering to so many lovers, Pisces will remain elusive. They are impossible to figure out ahead of time – today, they might be declaring their love for you, but tomorrow, they may disappear – possibly forever! To a Pisces, love is a fantasy, illusion, and dream, and they might spend their whole lives in pursuit of it. Pisces who are unhappy in love are vulnerable to alcoholism or drug addiction.

Cancer and Scorpio make the best partners for a Pisces. He is also easily dominated by Capricorn and Libra, but in turn will conquer even a queen-like Leo. Often, they are fascinated by Geminis – if they marry, it will last a long time, but likely not forever. Relationships with Aries and Sagittarians are erratic, though initially, things can seem almost perfect.

Women

ARIES

Aries women are leaders. They are decisive, bold, and very protective. An Aries can take initiative and is not afraid to make the first move. Her ideal man is strong, and someone she can admire. But remember, at the slightest whiff of weakness, she will knock him off his pedestal. She does not like dull, whiny men, and thinks that there is always a way out of any situation. If she loves someone, she will be faithful. Aries women are too honest to try leading a double life. They are possessive, jealous, and not only will they not forgive those who are unfaithful, their revenge may be brutal; they know no limits. If you can handle an Aries, don't try to put her in a cage; it is best to give her a long leash. Periodically give her some space – then she will seek you out herself. She is sexual, and believe that anything goes in bed.

Her best partners are a Sagittarius or Leo. A Libra can make a good match after middle age, once both partners have grown wiser and settled down a bit. Gemini and Aquarius are only good partners during the initial phase, when everything is still new, but soon enough, they will lose interest in each other. Scorpios are good matches in bed, but only suitable as lovers.

TAURUS

Taurean women possess qualities that men often dream about, but rarely find in the flesh – they are soft, charming, practical, and reliable – they are very caring and will support their partner in every way. A Taurus is highly sexual, affectionate, and can show a man how to take pleasure to new heights. She is also strong and intense. If she is in love, she will be faithful. But when love fades away, she might find someone else on the side, though she will still fight to save her marriage, particularly if her husband earns good money. A Taurus will not tolerate a man who is disheveled or disorganized, and anyone dating her needs to always be on his toes. She will expect gifts, and likes being taken to expensive restaurants, concerts, and other events. If you argue, try to make the first peace offering, because a Taurus finds it very hard to do so – she might withdraw and ruminate for a long time. Never air your dirty laundry; solve all your problems one-on-one.

Scorpio, Virgo, Capricorn, and Cancer make the best matches. A relationship with an Aries or Sagittarius would be difficult. There is little attraction between a Taurus and a Leo, and initially Libras can make for a good partner in bed, but things will quickly cool off and fall apart. A Taurus and Aquarius make an interesting match – despite the difference in signs, their relationships are often lasting, and almost lifelong.

GEMINI

Gemini women are social butterflies, outgoing, and they easily make friends, and then break off the friendship, if people do not hold their interest. A Gemini falls in love hard, is very creative, and often fantasizes about the object of her affection. She is uninterested in sex without any attachment, loves to flirt, and, for the most part, is not particularly affectionate. She dreams of a partner who is her friend, lover, and a romantic, all at once. A Gemini has no use for a man who brings nothing to the table intellectually. That is a tall order, so Geminis often divorce and marry several times. Others simply marry later in life. Once you have begun a life together, do not try to keep her inside – she needs to travel, explore, socialize, attend events and go to the theater. She cannot tolerate possessive men, so avoid giving her the third degree, and remember that despite her flirtatious and social nature, she is, in fact, faithful – as long as you keep her interested and she is in love. Astrologists believe that Geminis do not know what they need until age 29 or 30, so it is best to hold off on marriage until then.

Leo and Libra make the best matches. A relationship with a Cancer is likely, though complex, and depends solely on the Cancer's affection. A Gemini and Sagittarius can have an interesting, dynamic relationship, but these are two restless signs, which might only manage to get together after ages 40-45, once they have had enough thrills out of life and learned to be patient. Relationships with a Capricorn are very difficult, and almost never happen. The honeymoon stage can be wonderful with a Scorpio, but each partner will eventually go their own way, before ending things. A Gemini and Pisces union can also be very interesting – they are drawn to each other, and can have a wonderful relationship, but after a while, the cracks start to show and things will fall apart. An Aquarius is also not a bad match, but they will have little sexual chemistry.

CANCER

Cancers can be divided into two opposing groups. The first includes a sweet and gentle creature who is willing to dedicate her life to her husband and children. She is endlessly devoted to her husband, especially if he makes a decent living and remains faithful. She views all men as potential husbands, which means it is dangerous to strike up a relationship with her if your intentions are not serious; she can be anxious and clingy, sensitive and prone to crying. It is better to break things to her gently, rather than directly spitting out the cold, hard truth. She wants a man who can be a provider, though she often earns well herself. She puts money away for a rainy day, and knows how to be thrifty, for the sake of others around her, rather than only for herself. She is an excellent cook and capable of building an inviting home for her loved ones. She is enthusiastic in bed, a wonderful wife, and a caring mother.

The second type of Cancer is neurotic, and capable of creating a living hell for those around her. She believes that the world is her enemy, and manages to constantly find new intrigue and machinations.

Another Cancer, Virgo, Taurus, Scorpio, and Pisces make the best matches. A Cancer can often fall in love with a Gemini, but eventually, things will grow complicated, as she will be exhausted by a Gemini's constant mood swings and cheating. A Cancer and Sagittarius will initially have passionate sex, but things will quickly cool off. A relationship with a Capricorn is a real possibility, but only later in life, as while they are young, they are likely to fight and argue constantly. Cancer can also have a relationship with an Aries, but this will not be easy.

LEO

Leos are usually beautiful or charming, and outwardly sexual. And yet, appearances can be deceiving – they are not actually that interested in sex. Leo women want to be the center of attention and men running after them boosts their self-esteem, but they are more interested in their career, creating something new, and success than sex. They often have high-powered careers and are proud of their own achievements. Their partners need to be strong; if a Leo feels a man is weak, she can carry him herself for a while- before leaving him. It is difficult for her to find a partner for life, as chivalrous knights are a dying breed, and she is not willing to compromise. If you are interested in a Leo, take the initiative, admire her, and remember that even a queen is still a woman. Timid men or tightwads need not apply. Leos like to help others, but they don't need a walking disaster in their life. If they are married and in love, they are usually faithful, and petty gossip isn't their thing. Leo women make excellent mothers, and are ready to give their lives to their children. Their negative traits include vanity and a willingness to lie, in order to make themselves look better.

Sagittarius, Aries, and Libra make the best matches. Leos can also have an interesting relationship with a Virgo, though both partners will weaken each other. Life with a Taurus will lead to endless arguments – both signs are very stubborn, and unwilling to give in. Leos and Pisces are another difficult pair, as she will have to learn to be submissive if she wants to keep him around. A relationship with a Capricorn will work if there is a common denominator, but they will have little sexual chemistry. Life with a Scorpio will be turbulent to say the least, and they will usually break up later in life.

VIRGO

Virgo women are practical, clever, and often duplicitous. Marrying one isn't for everyone. She is a neat freak to the point of annoying those around her. She is also an excellent cook, and strives to ensure her children receive the very best by teaching them everything, and preparing them for a bright future. She is also thrifty – she won't throw money around, and, in fact, won't even give it to her husband. She has no time for rude, macho strongmen, and is suspicious of spendthrifts. She will not be offended if you take her to a cozy and modest café rather than an elegant restaurant. Virgos are masters of intrigue, and manage to outperform every other sign of the Zodiac in this regard. Virgos love to criticize everyone and everything; to listen to them, the entire world is simply a disaster and wrong, and only she is the exception to this rule. Virgos are not believed to be particularly sexual, but there are different variations when it comes to this. Rarely, one finds an open-minded Virgo willing to try anything, and who does it all on a grand scale – but she is rather the exception to this general rule.

The best matches for a Virgo are Cancer, Taurus, and Capricorn. She also can get along well with a Scorpio, but will find conflict with Sagittarius. A Pisces will strike her interest, but they will rarely make it down the aisle. She is often attracted to an Aquarius, but they would drive each other up the wall were they to actually marry. An Aries forces Virgo to see another side of life, but here, she will have to learn to conform and adapt.

LIBRA

Female Libras tend to be beautiful, glamorous, or very charming. They are practical, tactical, rational, though they are adept at hiding these qualities behind their romantic and elegant appearance. Libras are drawn to marriage, and are good at imagining the kind of partner they need. They seek out strong, well-off men and are often more interested in someone's social status and bank account than feelings. The object of their affection needs to be dashing, and have a good reputation in society. Libras love expensive things, jewelry, and finery. If they are feeling down, a beautiful gift will instantly cheer them up. They will not tolerate scandal or conflict, and will spend all their energy trying to keep the peace, or at least the appearance thereof. They do not like to air their dirty laundry, and will only divorce in extreme circumstances. They are always convinced they are right and react to any objections as though they have been insulted. Most Libras are not particularly sexual, except those with Venus or the Moon in Scorpio.

Leos, Geminis, and Aquarians make good matches. Libra women are highly attracted to Aries men - this is a real case of opposites attract. They can get along with a Sagittarius, though he will find that Libras are too proper and calm. Capricorn, Pisces, and Cancer are all difficult matches. Things will begin tumultuously with a Taurus, before each partner goes his or her own way.

SCORPIO

Scorpio women may appear outwardly restrained, but there is much more bubbling below the surface. They are ambitious with high self-esteem, but often wear a mask of unpretentiousness. They are the true power behind the scenes, the one who holds the family together, but never talk about it. Scorpios are strong-willed, resilient, and natural survivors. Often, Scorpios are brutally honest, and expect the same out of those around them. They do not like having to conform, and attempt to get others to adapt to them, as they honestly believe everyone will be better off that way. They are incredibly intuitive, and not easily deceived. They have an excellent memory, and can quickly figure out which of your buttons to push. They are passionate in bed, and their temperament will not diminish with age. When she is sexually frustrated, a Scorpio will throw all of her energy into her career or her loved ones. She is proud, categorical, and "if you don't do it right, don't do it at all" is her motto. Scorpio cannot be fooled, and she will not forgive any cheating. Will she cheat herself? Yes! But it will not break up her family, and she will attempt to keep it a secret. Scorpios are usually attractive to men, even if they are not particularly beautiful. They keep a low profile, though they always figure out their partner, and give them some invisible sign. There is also another, selfish type of Scorpio, who will use others for as long as they need them, before unceremoniously casting them aside.

Taurus is a good match; they will have excellent sexual chemistry and understand each other. Scorpio and Gemini are drawn to each other, but are unlikely to stay together long enough to actually get married. Cancer can be a good partner as well, but Cancers are possessive, while Scorpios do not like others meddling in their affairs, though they can later resolve their arguments in bed. Scorpio and Leo are often found together, but their relationship can also be very complicated. Leos are animated and chipper, while Scorpios, who are much deeper and more stubborn, see Leos as not particularly serious or reliable. One good example of this is Bill (a Leo) and Hillary (a Scorpio) Clinton. Virgo can also make a good partner, but when Scorpio seemingly lacks emotions, he will look for them elsewhere. Relationships with Lira are strange and very rare. Scorpio sees Libra as too insecure, and Libra does not appreciate Scorpio's rigidity. Two Scorpios together make an excellent marriage! Sagittarius and Scorpio are unlikely to get together, as she will think he is shallow and rude. If they do manage to get married, Scorpio's drive and persistence is the only thing that will make the marriage last. Capricorn is also not a bad match, and while Scorpio finds Aquarius attractive, they will rarely get married, as they are simply speaking different languages! Things are alright with a Pisces, as both signs are emotional, and Pisces can let Scorpio take the lead when necessary.

SAGITTARIUS

Sagittarius women are usually charming, bubbly, energetic, and have the gift of gab. They are kind, sincere, and love people. They are also straightforward, fair, and very ambitious, occasionally to the point of irritating those around them. But telling them something is easier than not telling them, and they often manage to win over their enemies. Sagittarius tends to have excellent intuition, and she loves to both learn and teach others. She is a natural leader, and loves taking charge at work and at home. Many Sagittarian women have itchy feet, and prefer all kinds of travel to sitting at home. They are not particularly good housewives – to be frank, cooking and cleaning is simply not for them. Their loved ones must learn to adapt to them, but Sagittarians themselves hate any pressure. They are not easy for men to handle, as Sagittarians want to be in charge. Sagittarius falls in love easily, is very sexual and temperamental, and may marry multiple times. Despite outward appearances, Sagittarius is a very lonely sign. Even after she is married with children, she may continue living as if she were alone; you might say she marches to the beat of her own drum. Younger

Sagittarians can be reckless, but as they mature, they can be drawn to religion, philosophy, and the occult.

Aries and Leo make the best matches, as Sagittarius is able to bend to Leo's ways, or at least pretend to. Sagittarians often end up with Aquarians, but their marriages do not tend to be for the long haul. They are attracted to Geminis, but are unlikely to marry one until middle age, when both signs have settled down. Sagittarius and Cancer have incredible sexual chemistry, but an actual relationship between them would be tumultuous and difficult. Capricorn can make a good partner- as long as they are able to respect each other's quirks. Sagittarius rarely ends up with a Virgo, and while she may often meet Pisces, things are unlikely to go very far.

CAPRICORN

Capricorn women are conscientious, reliable, organized, and hard-working. Many believe that life means nothing but work, and live accordingly. They are practical, and not particularly drawn to parties or loud groups of people. But if someone useful will be there, they are sure to make an appearance. Capricorn women are stingy, but not as much as their male counterparts. They are critical of others, but think highly of themselves. Generally, they take a difficult path in life, but thanks to their dedication, perseverance, and willingness to push their own limits, they are able to forge their own path, and by 45 or 50, they can provide themselves with anything they could want. Capricorn women have the peculiarity of looking older than their peers when they are young, and younger than everyone else once they have matured. They are not particularly sexual, and tend to be faithful partners. They rarely divorce, and even will fight until the end, even for a failed marriage. Many Capricorns have a pessimistic outlook of life, and have a tendency to be depressed. They are rarely at the center of any social circle, but are excellent organizers. They have a very rigid view of life and love, and are not interested in a fling, as marriage is the end goal. As a wife, Capricorn is simultaneously difficult and reliable. She is difficult because of her strict nature and difficulty adapting. But she will also take on all the household duties, and her husband can relax, knowing his children are in good hands.

Taurus, Pisces, and Scorpio make good matches. Aries is difficult, once things cool off after the initial honeymoon. When a Capricorn meets another Capricorn, they will be each other's first and last love. Sagittarius isn't a bad match, but they don't always pass the test of time. Aquarius and Capricorn are a difficult match, and rarely found together. Things are too dull with a Virgo, and while Leo can be exciting at first, things will fall apart when he begins showing off. Libra and Aquarius are both difficult partners for Capricorn, and she is rarely found with either of them.

AQUARIUS

A female Aquarius is very different from her male counterparts. She is calm and keeps a cool head, but she is also affectionate and open. She values loyalty above all else, and is unlikely to recover from any infidelity, though she will only divorce if this becomes a chronic trend, and she has truly been stabbed in the back. She is not interested in her partner's money, but rather, his professional success. She is unobtrusive and trusting, and will refrain from listening in on her partner's phone conversations or hacking into his email. With rare exceptions, Aquarian women make terrible housewives. But they are excellent partners in life – they are faithful, never boring, and will not reject a man, even in the most difficult circumstances. Most Aquarians are highly intuitive, and can easily tell the truth from a lie. They themselves only lie in extreme situations, which call for a "white lie" in order to avoid hurting someone's feelings.

Aquarius gets along well with Aries, Gemini, and Libra. She can also have a good relationship with a Sagittarius. Taurus often makes a successful match, though they are emotionally very different; the same goes for Virgo. Aquarius and Scorpio, Capricorn, or Cancer is a difficult match. Pisces can make a good partner as well, as both signs complement each other. Any relationship with a Leo will be tumultuous, but lasting, as Leo is selfish, and Aquarius will therefore have to be very forgiving.

PISCES

Pisces women are very adaptable, musically inclined, and erotic. They possess an innate earthly wisdom, and a good business sense. Pisces often reinvent themselves; they can be emotional, soft, and obstinate, as well as sentimental, at times. Their behavioral changes can be explained by frequent ups and downs. Pisces is charming, caring, and her outward malleability is very attractive to men. She is capable of loving selflessly, as long as the man has something to love. Even if he doesn't, she will try and take care of him until the very end. Pisces' greatest fear is poverty. They are intuitive, vulnerable, and always try to avoid conflict. They love to embellish the truth, and sometimes alcohol helps with this. Rarely, one finds extremely unbalanced, neurotic and dishonest Pisces, who are capable of turning their loved ones' lives into a living Hell!

Taurus, Capricorn, Cancer, and Scorpio make the best matches. She will be greatly attracted to a Virgo, but a lasting relationship is only likely if both partners are highly spiritual. Any union with a Libra is likely to be difficult and full of conflict. Pisces finds Gemini attractive, and they may have a very lively relationship – for a while. Occasionally, Pisces ends up with a Sagittarius, but she will have to fade into the background and entirely submit to him. If she ends up with an Aquarius, expect strong emotional outbursts, and a marriage that revolves around the need to raise their children.

Tatiana Borsch

Made in the USA
Middletown, DE
27 September 2020